WRITING SU[...]
ACADEMIC[...]

'Publish or perish' is a well-established adage in academia. Never has the pressure on academics to publish been greater. Yet the prospect of writing a book can seem daunting, while the business of getting it published may be mystifying. Written by an expert in academic publishing, *Writing Successful Academic Books* provides a practical guide to both writing and getting published. It covers all stages of academic authorship from developing the initial idea for a book through to post-publication issues, showing how to avoid the common pitfalls and achieve academic and professional success through publication. Full of real-life examples, including a sample book proposal, the book covers everything you need to know to build up an authorial career. This is an invaluable guide for academic authors – prospective or established – in all disciplines.

ANTHONY HAYNES is Director of The Professional and Higher Partnership Ltd, where he specialises in academic publishing. He is Visiting Professor at Beijing Normal University, China, teaches academic authorship online at the University of Tartu, Estonia, and mentors numerous academic authors in the UK. He holds qualifications from Cambridge University, the Open University, and the University of Malta. His previous books include *Writing Successful Textbooks*.

WRITING SUCCESSFUL ACADEMIC BOOKS

ANTHONY HAYNES

CAMBRIDGE
UNIVERSITY PRESS

CAMBRIDGE UNIVERSITY PRESS
Cambridge, New York, Melbourne, Madrid, Cape Town, Singapore,
São Paulo, Delhi, Dubai, Tokyo

Cambridge University Press
The Edinburgh Building, Cambridge CB2 8RU, UK

Published in the United States of America by Cambridge University Press, New York

www.cambridge.org
Information on this title: www.cambridge.org/9780521730747

First published 2010

Printed in the United Kingdom at the University Press, Cambridge

A catalogue record for this publication is available from the British Library

Library of Congress Cataloguing in Publication data
Haynes, Anthony.
Writing successful academic books / Anthony Haynes.
p.   cm.
ISBN 978-0-521-51498-9 (hardback)
1. Authorship.   2. Academic writing.   3. Scholarly publishing.   I. Title.
PN146.H375 2010
808′.02–dc22
2009053429
ISBN 978-0-521-51498-9 Hardback
ISBN 978-0-521-73074-7 Paperback

To Karen, Frances, Jonty, and Simon

Contents

Figures

Tables

Boxes

Foreword

Experienced editor and Visiting Professor at Beijing Normal University Anthony Haynes has provided a highly useful guide for authors of academic books. Authors are very competent in their specialism; however, they may encounter problems in negotiations with the publisher, in presenting their material in book form, etc. Anthony Haynes shares his broad competence on all the stages of writing and editing academic books.

Often academicians have trouble answering the question 'Should I write a book?' Professor Haynes erases all doubt, indicating that writing a book is a part of self-realisation, it raises one's self-esteem, and fosters career development. Thereafter he leads the author through the process of writing.

Anthony Haynes explains how to evoke an editor's interest in asking you to write a book. He writes in lively detail on how to compose a book proposal and gives an example, which includes an interesting analysis of competing titles. In the proposal, one has to indicate who will buy the book and why, as well as make decisions about the style of presenting content.

The writing process begins with the incubation of ideas and planning. Professor Haynes explains the pros and cons of linear and non-linear planning, gives hints for the division of chapters into subsections, using questions in plans, and composing a word budget. He stresses the idea that you should not do too much self-editing while first drafting your book. The process of redrafting is also very important, and effective ways for redrafting are depicted. Interesting ideas about the opening sentence of a paragraph and the tone of writing are presented. The most important problems with tables and figures are indicated and solutions proposed. Useful recommendations on writing dissertations, time management while writing a book, and working with editors are then covered.

Professor Haynes has provided a complete treatment of what an author needs to know to write an academic book. His work is a practical guide that enables authors to achieve their aims more efficiently. It differs from other analogous titles in having good examples, lively style, and practice-related content.

JAAN MIKK

Professor Emeritus
University of Tartu, Estonia

Preface

Two motivations lie behind this book. I would like to pass on what I have learnt from working with a number of successful academic authors; and I'd like to help authors to avoid the problems that recur, often all too predictably, in academic writing and publishing. In attempting to do so, I draw on my professional experience as editor and publisher, as author, and as a trainer or mentor of authors in a number of universities. In a sense, then, this book is a work of reportage.

The word 'successful' in the title of this book is deliberately ambiguous. The text is concerned with success both in writing books – in getting them written as well as possible – and in having them published as well as possible. By focusing on both types of success, the book seeks to build a bridge between the worlds of publishing and academia. In its attempt to make sense of one world on behalf of the other, this book is also a work of interpretation.

The chapters are grouped, loosely, into three parts. The first part ('Becoming an Author') provides a launchpad. It examines such questions as: Why write? What to write? Where to publish? With what reward? The focus is on success in publishing. The second part, 'Writing the Text', is most concerned with 'how' questions: how to generate ideas, work with language, shape the text, and so on. The focus is on success in writing. In the third part, 'Managing the Project', the main concern is again with 'how' questions – how to manage time, work with other people involved with your book, and manage your authorial career. There the focus is fairly evenly divided between success in writing and success in publication.

I should say a word about the notes. I dislike poky superscript numbers and the requirement they inflict on readers to flick to and fro between main text and endnotes, so I have decided to spare my readers. Whenever the title of a book is cited in the text, you will find the work listed in the references towards the back of this book. Details of the other sources mentioned in the text are given in the endnotes. The notes also include some recommendations for further reading. In return for trying to make the notes readable and keep them concise, I hereby challenge my publishers to print them in the same size font as the main text.

I am grateful to Frances Haynes for reading the text and providing perceptive comments. I am also grateful to Robert Yarwood (Authors' Licensing and Collecting Society), James Willis (Association of Authors' Agents) and Paul Machen (Society of Indexers) for responding to queries.

Given the subject matter of this book, I should perhaps add, for the avoidance of doubt, that the views expressed in these pages are my own and not necessarily those of my publisher.

PART I

Becoming an Author

CHAPTER I

Foundations

If you are reading this page, the likelihood is either that you have decided to write an academic book or that you are contemplating doing so. The decision to write a book entails a number of questions. For example: Why write? What to write? For whom? And what does one want to achieve? These are the questions this chapter is designed to answer.

WHY WRITE?

Writing a book is a serious commitment, one that is likely to require several hundred hours of your time. It is worth examining, therefore, the reasons for making that commitment. There is, after all, no shortage of other things one can do with one's time.

I suspect that many academic authors don't give much thought to the question, 'Why write?' The phrase 'publish or perish' is well established in academia and it is tempting to treat it as a sufficient answer to our question. Yet it's worth going behind this phrase and considering the question of authorial motivation in more detail. Aims vary greatly between authors. The more conscious you are of your aims, the more you can use them to guide the decisions you make as an author – and the more likely you are to achieve those aims.

Let's consider some of the typical motivations. First, there is the wish to make money. This is a motivation that academic authors often play down. As an acquisitions editor, I have often enjoyed conversations with prospective authors along the following lines:

ME: Now, we need to discuss royalty rates.
AUTHOR: Yes – though of course I'm not doing this for the money, you realise.

ME: Oh, well, in that case we can deal with this very easily. Let's just write in the contract that royalties shall be payable to me instead of you.

Strangely enough, at this point authors always decide that actually they are interested in the money after all! I should add that as an editor I rather welcome this, since it encourages commitment on the part of the author. Professionalism is welcome.

The main means by which academic authors earn an income directly from their books is the royalty. This is a payment based on the number of copies sold. It is calculated as a percentage, either of list price or net receipts. For example, if the publisher announces a list (i.e. retail) price of £30 and the author is on a royalty rate of 10 per cent of list price, the author will earn £3 for each copy sold. If, on the other hand, the royalty rate is 10 per cent of net receipts, the author will earn 10 per cent of whatever the publisher receives from the sale of the book. Suppose, for instance, the retailer buys the book from the publisher at 50 per cent discount: the publisher will receive, in this example, £50 and the author will therefore earn £5. (Not surprisingly, the percentage rates that publishers offer on list price royalties tend to be lower than those that they offer on a net receipt basis.)

Sometimes publishers will offer a fee rather than a royalty. This arrangement is most common in reference publishing, where a large project such as an encyclopaedia may have hundreds, or even thousands, of contributors and royalty payments would be complicated. From the author's point of view, the payment of a fee instead of a royalty is likely to prove attractive in the short term, offering payment – possibly of quite a reasonable sum – early in the process, but less attractive long term (precisely because the fee is a one-off payment).

In addition, authors may earn money from their books through the sale of subsidiary rights. For example, a newspaper or magazine may pay for the right to publish extracts from the book. This is known as serialisation. The proceeds are usually split between the publisher and the author according to percentages stipulated in the publishing contract. Serialisation rights can be substantial: in the case of national publications, sums running to four or five figures are not unusual. For academics, these are most likely to accrue in the case of 'trade crossover' books – that is, books that originate from academic work but cross over into a more general consumer market.

A more common source of subsidiary rights earnings from academic books is the sale of translation rights. An Anglophone publisher may, for example, sell to another publisher the right to translate into another language. Payment usually comes in the form of a royalty, again split between the original publisher and the author.

The sums involved in translation rights are often small. Most of the deals that I have been involved in have yielded a few hundred dollars, split equally between publisher and author. However, such payments often provide authors with a welcome bonus. After all, they usually require no additional input from the author, beyond the original writing of the book, and often arrive out of the blue, long after the book has been written. It can be surprising which languages books get translated into. Several books that I've worked on have been translated into eastern European languages in territories with small populations. Authors of academic books often derive as much satisfaction from the knowledge that their books are being read internationally as they do from the earnings that follow.

In addition to payments from publishers, in the form of royalties, fees, and subsidiary rights, authors may earn an income from secondary rights. This source of income is not as well known as it should be. It comprises royalty payments for such activities as photocopying or broadcasting a work, sometimes occurring years or even decades after the work was originally published. Typically, such sums are collected centrally by a national body and then distributed to authors, provided they subscribe to the collecting organisation. Such arrangements now operate in dozens of countries. If you are a published author, I recommend that you consider subscribing and registering your works: you may well find you are already entitled to some money! The relevant organisation in the UK is the Authors' Licensing and Collecting Society (ALCS). US residents may also register with ALCS. Details of organisations in other territories may be obtained from the International Confederation of Societies for Authors and Composers (CISAC) and International Federation of Reproduction Rights Organisations (IFRRO).

In addition to direct earnings, academics often derive an income from authorships indirectly. Having one's book published may lead, for example, to invitations to speak, appear in the media, or write articles. It is not at all unusual for such income to amount to more than the direct earnings from the book itself. If being published leads to an offer of consultancy projects or perhaps even a better job, the return (in terms of lifetime earnings) on your investment (i.e. the hours spent writing the book) may be very high indeed. Even if financial remuneration is not your main motivation, it does no harm to be alert to the opportunities.

A very different kind of motivation is altruism. When Lord Reith was Director General of the BBC, he believed that its mission was to 'inform, educate, and entertain'. That famous phrase – especially the first two-thirds of it – encapsulates the mission of many academic authors too. In book proposals, such a mission may be expressed either in positive form – an author may wish to publish their research findings in order to stimulate more enlightened public policy, for example – or more negatively (in terms of, say, demythologising a subject or exposing fallacies or inconsistencies in conventional wisdom). Either way, the desire to enlighten is certainly a common motivation in academic authorship.

Altruism and the desire for financial gain are often spoken of as if they stood at opposite ends of a spectrum. Indeed, they're sometimes seen as incompatible: mammon is suspected of corrupting the desire to enlighten. Yet this need not be the case. Often, in fact, the two motivations are not merely compatible, but mutually reinforcing. After all, a book for which there is no market is no use to anyone: however much wisdom it may contain, it will go to waste if the book goes unread. In contrast, a highly marketable book may enlighten many readers.

Another common motivation to write is the desire to learn. Publishing an academic book provides the author with a variety of learning opportunities. In the first place, the author learns through the process of composition. Often, it's while actually writing that one learns what it is one wants to say. Second, one learns from having one's book published something about the way that the publishing industry works. One may learn, for example, about processes, such as proofreading and indexing, and about the work of others, such as copy-editors and designers. This knowledge, which authors sometimes find interesting itself, may be applied in one's subsequent work as an author and in mentoring colleagues who are new to the business of publishing. Finally, and often most importantly, one learns from feedback from readers – formally, through reviews and critiques, and informally, through comments and personal communications. As an author, you learn, bracingly, about the errors and weaknesses in one's work; you learn too, frustratingly but usefully, about the way people misunderstand your work; and you learn about what people find interesting in your work. This may prove stimulating: what other people find interesting might be neither what interested you nor what you had thought would interest your readers.

A different kind of motivation is the desire to raise one's esteem. Being published at someone else's expense provides evidence that someone else, besides yourself, regards your work as valuable – valuable enough to invest thousands of pounds and many hours of attentive labour. It also provides visible, tangible, evidence of achievement to those around you who might not be part of the academic world – your partner, parents, children, and so on.

There are qualitative and quantitative components to the esteem that derives from authorship. The former result from the quality of your work and of your publisher. The higher the publisher's standards – especially in terms of commissioning, editing, and book production – the greater the esteem. The quantitative aspect of authorial esteem results from the number of readers that your book attracts. That too is a product of both your own labours and the publisher's.

To such esteem should be added that of another kind, namely self-esteem. Many authors derive a good, old-fashioned, sense of satisfaction from seeing their name in print on the cover of the product of a reputable press. I vividly recall the thrill on seeing a copy of my first book, published by A&C Black, for the first time. Though it may not be on a par with getting married or becoming a parent, I'd certainly rate the experience right at the top of the second division.

A further motivation for authors, one closely connected to that of raising esteem, is the desire to develop one's career. The significance of book authorship on an academic CV varies considerably between countries and between disciplines. In some systems, in some disciplines, book authorship is a more or less formal requirement for tenure, featuring as either 'desirable' or 'essential' in the list of criteria used by appointment committees. In many other contexts, the contribution of authorship to one's prospects is less formal, but nonetheless positive. A book can provide direct, readily obtainable, evidence of your productivity and scholarship. In addition, it can help to get your name known even amongst those who have not read your book. Sometimes, indeed, it is the magnum opus in the form of a heavyweight book that secures for its author a prestigious chair.

There may, then, be many reasons why you might wish to write an academic book: you may wish, directly or indirectly, to make money; to spread enlightenment; to learn more; to raise your esteem; or to enhance your career prospects. And the fact that good reasons exist for wanting to write academic books leads to one final reason. It is certainly the case that if, as an academic author, you wish to be published, it helps considerably if you have been published before. One good reason for writing one academic book, therefore, is simply that it helps you win a publishing contract for the next one.

WHAT TO WRITE

The question of what to write is in part a question of content. That is, it may in part be answered by considering which topics you will cover, which questions you will seek to answer, which data you will include, etc. But the question of what to write requires decisions not only about content, but also about genre. As an acquisitions editor I have read countless book proposals from academic authors. Very few of them have failed to tell me enough about the proposed contents of their books. Many of them, however, have failed to make clear what genre the authors thought the books in question belonged to. When I have pursued this matter, I have found that on occasion this is a matter of oversight – the author is clear what genre the proposed book belongs to but has failed to provide an explicit statement, perhaps in the belief that the fact is self-evident. But on other occasions I've found that the reason authors have failed to clarify the question of genre in their proposals is that they are not clear about it themselves.

Let's get clear why genre matters. Genre is what might be called a 'macro-level' description of a piece of writing. It is a description of what type of work we are dealing with. We might say of a certain book that it is, for example, a 'monograph' or a 'reader'. Each genre is characterised by a set of conventions. These conventions are not hard-and-fast rules. They are, rather, guidelines, corresponding to the expectations that users – whether readers, editors, librarians, or indeed authors – bring to the work.

Decisions about genre tend to be powerful. Suppose an author is trying to decide whether a putative book is best thought of as a monograph, aimed at scholarly readers, or a popular book, aimed at the consumer book market. Once the decision over genre has been made, the author will find that many other authorial decisions immediately become clearer. For example:

- What level should the argument be pitched at?
- Who am I writing for?
- How much knowledge on the part of the reader may I assume?
- How formal should the style be?
- How much jargon can I use?
- What tone should I use?
- How much data should I include?
- How many footnotes and references should I provide?

Clarity about genre is, then, a helpful thing for an author to have: it makes the book more writable.

Let us, briefly, survey the major academic genres. When I was working as a publishing director for a company that published several hundred titles a year, I decided to categorise the output by genre. I found that the majority of titles could be distributed into four categories, namely (a) reference works, (b) monographs, (c) adoptables, and (d) trade books. Let's look at each of these in turn.

Reference works are typically texts that are designed to be consulted every now and then, rather than read through from cover to cover. They include encyclopaedias, bibliographies, and dictionaries. The main organising principle in reference works is usually neither narrative nor argument: principles such as alphabetical order, chronology or logical hierarchy are used instead. Usually what we might call the architecture of the work is made very explicit. Though reference works vary considerably in length, they are often very long. Partly for that reason, they tend to be written by teams of contributors – often scores or even hundreds. These days it is rare for an academic reference work to be published only in print. It is likely to be published electronically as well – or, as is increasingly the case, in electronic format alone. Reference works can be expensive. Prices running to several hundreds, or even thousands, of dollars are not uncommon. Typically, libraries constitute the main market for academic reference works.

A good, indeed wonderful, example of such a work is the 2004 edition of the *Oxford Dictionary of National Biography*. The print version runs to sixty volumes. Written by over 10,000 contributors, it includes well over 50,000 biographical articles. The print edition is organised alphabetically and has retailed at US$6,500 (though, at the time of writing, the publisher is experimenting with a reduced price). The online edition, which continues to grow as new articles are added, is sold on subscription. It is searchable in numerous ways (for example by person's name, place name, or key word).

Not all reference works are published on such a monumental scale. In recent years there has been a burgeoning of single-volume 'soft reference' titles published in series. For example, Blackwell and Cambridge University Press each publish extensive series of 'companions', whilst Oxford University Press publishes a series of 'handbooks'. Books in these series typically consist of hundreds rather than thousands of pages, and the paperback editions at least are priced for individual purchase (usually well under £100).

A second genre in academic publishing is the monograph. The term 'monograph' is difficult to define. Originally, it referred to a treatise in natural history devoted to an account of a single species, genus, or class of natural object. During the nineteenth century the meaning of the term began to broaden. In particular, it started to cross disciplines. Now the term means something more like 'a treatise or study of a specialised kind'. In academia the term is sometimes used to mean no more than a free-standing essay. Universities occasionally produce 'monograph' series comprising photocopied works each of twenty pages or so, either stapled or ring-bound. Usually, however, 'monograph' refers to something more substantial. Most monographs published in book form come in somewhere near the middle of the 50,000- to 100,000-word range. Monographs are written by, and usually for, scholars, researchers, or professional experts. The hallmark of a monograph is specialist expertise. Without that, a monograph is no sort of book at all.

Monographs are a staple of academic book publishing. Many scholars have begun their book publishing careers with books derived from their doctoral dissertations. Some sign off their careers with monographs condensing a lifetime of learning devoted to a single field. Books in this genre are usually published in hardback and/or as e-books. Sometimes there is a paperback too, perhaps published subsequently. For hardbacks and e-books, prices of close to, or over, £100 are common. The library sector is an important market for such books.

A third genre (or, we shall see, group of genres) consists of adoptables. You may well not have encountered this term as a noun before. The *OED* does not list it as such, and I rather hope I may lay claim to coining it. By 'adoptable', I mean a book that is suitable for adoption by lecturers. That is, a book that is recommended to students for use on an academic course.

The most obvious form of adoptable is the textbook. The *OED* defines a 'text-book' as: 'A book used as a standard work for the study of a particular subject; now usually one written specially for this purpose; a manual of instruction in any science or branch of study, esp. a work recognized as an authority'.

This definition feels slightly jaded. For current usage, 'recommended' might be happier than 'standard'. One virtue of the definition, however, is that it is wide enough to encompass many sorts of text, including both (a) standard editions (such as the texts of classic works in philosophy published by Hackett) and (b) expository works. The latter include such famous texts as *Economics* by Paul Samuelson, *Business Accounting* by Frank Wood, and *Principles Of Marketing* by Philip Kotler. The hallmark of this latter type is clear, well-organised, expository prose. This may be accompanied, to a greater or lesser extent, by pedagogical apparatus, such as statements of desired learning outcomes, case studies, questions, exercises and activities, and guidance on further study. The modern era has seen a trend towards greater provision of such features. Where the pedagogical apparatus predominates, as in many English-as-a-foreign-language texts, the term 'coursebook' is usually preferred.

The *OED*'s definition also recognises that not all textbooks are purpose-written. Some books get adopted simply because they are the most appropriate available. This happens most in fields that are relatively new or small. In tourism studies, for example, some of the books published by Channel View that might normally be regarded as monographs seem to have been adopted because of an absence of genuine textbooks for some modules.

Successful textbooks sell year after year and are frequently updated. Their sales are strongly seasonal, with peaks at the beginning of semesters (especially at the start of the academic year) and troughs in university vacation periods.

A second form of adoptable is that of the reader. This is a collection of articles or essays by diverse hands. Sometimes the texts are specially commissioned, though usually they are previously published. Indeed, texts are often included in readers precisely because they have been influential and may even have assumed classic status. Often readers are developed in order to supplement textbooks. For example, in communication studies Sage publish a textbook written by Denis McQuail (*McQuail's Mass Communication Theory*) and an accompanying reader, compiled by McQuail (*McQuail's Reader in Mass Communication Theory*). Readers such as these serve to introduce students directly to primary sources and provide a wider range of voice and perspective than does the single-authored textbook.

A third, more amorphous, type of adoptable is the student guide. These tend to be shorter, less comprehensive, and lower-priced than textbooks. Often the tone is informal and friendly. See, for example, the various series of student guides published by Continuum. For instance, books in the Key Concepts series each introduce students to a single concept or set of concepts (such as 'logic' or 'epistemology'); those in the Reader's Guides series help students to read classic texts (Kant's *Critique of Pure Reason*, for example); whilst books in the Guides for the Perplexed series usually introduce students to key thinkers (Wittgenstein, for example). Students often welcome the encouraging, supportive tone of such guides, whilst academic authors often welcome the opportunity they provide to 'sell' their subject. This is predominantly a paperback market. Student guides sometimes achieve sales beyond the academic market.

The final genre we will consider here is trade crossover books. This phrase, like 'adoptables', is really an umbrella term, covering a range of genres (including biography, polemic, travelogue, memoir, and even coffee-table books). They are books written by academics but marketed to consumers beyond academia.

Such books are sometimes referred to by phrases with a derogatory feel to them, such as 'pot-boiler'. They can provoke a mixture of academic snobbery and derision amongst those who haven't been invited to write them. I can, however, see nothing unrespectable about wanting to communicate with people beyond the campus (many of whom, after all, fund academia through their taxes). In fact, to popularise a subject well is no simple task and typically requires an understanding on the part of the author that is both clear and profound. Great popularisers such as Bertrand Russell and Stephen Jay Gould do not seem to have been intellectual lightweights.

As an acquisitions editor, I have long since lost count of the number of book proposals I have received from academic authors assuring me that they can write 'accessibly' for the popular market. Often the very style of the proposals, full of convoluted sentences crammed with jargon, indicates that the opposite is true. In any case, accessibility is only a necessary condition for popularisation, not a sufficient one. Readers need to be engaged and entertained – and to feel that what they are reading matters. This is a difficult brief to master, but it can be done. For inspiration, I suggest looking at Penguin Books' publishing programme (especially its Allen Lane list), which is replete with crossover books by academics such as James Watson, Stephen Hawking, Steven Pinker, and Robin Lane Fox.

The taxonomy that I have used here – reference works, monographs, adoptables, and trade crossover books – isn't exhaustive. In particular, I have ignored the genre known as 'supplementary texts'. These are texts that might get onto course reading lists, but not as the main text. They fall under the rubric of 'wider reading'. Typically, they fall somewhere between textbooks and monographs, lacking the teachability or learnability of the former and the depth or rigour of the latter. Not infrequently, they are edited collections, sometimes beginning life as sets of conference papers.

I have ignored them here for the same reason that I deliberately omitted them from the taxonomy I devised as a publishing director, which is that I don't believe in them. Supplementary books all too often fall betwixt and between: the book proposals that support them typically allude to student sales that never materialise, whilst libraries too, for one reason or another, tend not to see them as must-haves (the books may be seen as too ephemeral or too tangential).

Supplementary texts do get published, especially by small university presses and independent publishers, but for every one that succeeds there are dozens that fail. If the book that you are considering writing is in truth a supplementary text, then approaching one of these presses is certainly an option. My advice, however, would be first to ask yourself whether you really want to write the book and to be sure that there is a convincing answer to the question that sales managers, library suppliers, and retailers will undoubtedly ask: 'Who needs it?'

Earlier I suggested that thinking about the question of genres is a helpful thing for authors to do. It helps with decisions over what books to write and how to write them. It is also important when it comes to publishing. Think of publishing as a series of channels linking publishers and markets. There are, for example, monograph channels: they are efficient at getting books out of publishers' warehouses and onto library shelves, via library suppliers. They might also be efficient at getting review copies into the hands of reviews editors for learned journals. Textbook channels, on the other hand, are designed to be efficient first at getting marketing information, followed by inspection copies, into the hands of lecturers who teach courses, and then getting copies into campus bookstores when the books get adopted. And so for each genre: each has its own combination of channels. It is crucial, therefore, to ensure that it is clear which genre the book you write belongs to, otherwise it will get sent down the wrong channels and will not end up in the right hands. Which is to say, it won't get bought and it won't get read.

SUMMARY

1. Seek to clarify your motivation for writing.
2. In particular, consider the importance of: financial reward; altruism; learning; the author's esteem; and career development.
3. Decide which genre you propose to write in.
4. In particular, decide whether your book is intended as a reference work, monograph, adoptable (textbook, reader, or student guide), or trade crossover book (or whether it is a supplementary text).
5. Clarifying the genre will help you to write the book ...
6. ... and your publisher to market and sell it.

CHAPTER 2

Contexts

John Donne famously wrote that 'No man is an island.' Certainly no author is. Though writing may at times be a solitary business, getting published certainly isn't. Publishing introduces the work of the author into a busy, crowded landscape. The purpose of this chapter is to survey the publishing scene to see how it is populated – and how it is changing.

THE PUBLISHING SCENE

There are many different types of publishers. Here we will begin to differentiate them. Later, in Chapter 3 (see pp. 31–3), we will consider in more detail why it matters which company you publish with and how to go about selecting a publisher.

Over the years I have listened to many authors discuss publishers and the differences between them. In the conversations, two variables commonly feature, namely (1) the size of the publishing house, and (2) its provenance. Let's consider size first.

Differences in size between academic publishers can be extreme. At one end of the spectrum are multinational conglomerates, often themselves part of even larger media empires. Routledge, for example, is part of Taylor & Francis, which, in turn, is part of Informa. As I write (late Febuary 2009, following a stock market crash), Informa is valued on the London Stock Exchange at just over £900 million. Reed Elsevier is valued at nearly £6 billion and Pearson at over £5 billion. At the other end of the spectrum are a number of microbusinesses. My favourite example is a company I came across at a conference on educational leadership: it had four titles and one author. Exact figures for many academic publishers are hard to come by, simply because their revenue falls below the threshold that would require them to publish detailed accounts. That fact itself, however, tells us what we need to know. Many publishers in the sector have revenues of less than £10 million, placing them firmly at the 'small' end of the 'small and medium enterprise' (SME) category. Ashgate, for example, is a successful, well-known, transatlantic publisher of monographs, yet the most recent set of accounts indicate a revenue (for 2007) of just over £5 million.

Large publishing companies are able to take advantage of economies of scale, which in the publishing industry may be considerable. As a result, there are undoubtedly some advantages to be gained from publishing with a large company. Large companies simply have more clout than small ones. This makes it easier for them to get their books into the supply chain. That is, they are more able to persuade retailers, wholesalers, library suppliers, and stockists to handle their goods. They are also likely to obtain better terms. Their market position gives them muscle when it comes to negotiating discounts with their clients – an important consideration for those authors paid on net receipts royalties (see p. 4).

Large companies also tend to have more specialised staff. For example, they will have sales staff dedicated to export sales and even to specific export territories. They will also have rights specialists who will, for example, attend major book fairs such as Frankfurt and London in order to sell translation and co-publishing rights to other publishers. Large publishers are usually better at ensuring that their titles are readily available in more parts of the world than are the minnows.

Large publishers also have some advantages in marketing. The larger the publishing programme, the more opportunities there are for cross-marketing – the more conferences the publishers attend, the more marketing pieces they will mail or e-mail, and the more potential customers they will know through their sales data.

Publishers frequently allow their authors to buy books (any books, not just an author's own work) at a discount. If you buy a lot of books from a particular publisher in your field, the saving may be considerable. I have heard some authors say that this saving is worth more to them than their royalties.

Note that many of the advantages to authors and their books accrue automatically, without anyone giving their particular titles any special attention. This is just as well, since the lack of such attention is often one of the disadvantages of publishing with a large company. If your publishers publish hundreds or thousands of titles a year, and have vastly more titles on the backlist, your own work may struggle to gain attention from sales and marketing departments. It is a fact of life that publishers devote more resources (in fact, disproportionately more) to a small number of best-selling titles. The majority of their authors, therefore, will find that their books occupy relatively unimportant places in their publishers' programmes.

The advantages and disadvantages of publishing with a small company are to a large extent simply the flipside of those pertaining to publishing with large companies. A small Western publisher is unlikely, for example, to attend the Beijing Book Fair and so probably won't do many rights deals with Chinese presses. More importantly, they may struggle to gain respect, or even attention, from retail chains such as Barnes & Noble, or from the literary editors of national newspapers or magazines. On the other hand, a run-of-the-mill academic text may gain more attention from the editorial and marketing staff of a small press than it would from those of a large one: in a smaller programme, each title counts for more. Moreover – and this is probably the main advantage that small presses can offer – small companies may be very effective niche players. They may develop a detailed understanding of specialist markets that large publishers regard as too small to concern themselves with.

When it comes to authors' preferences, the choice between large and small publishers is often a question of temperament. Some authors prefer to be small fish in large ponds, others to be large fish in small pools. Unless, however, you happen to be a large fish in a large pond, it is difficult to enjoy all of the potential advantages of authorship at the same time: often there is a trade-off between economies of scale, on the one hand, and specialist handling on the other.

Along with size, the other key variable between publishers is provenance. In academia, many people draw a distinction between not-for-profit publishers (university presses, say, or learned societies) and commercial presses (whether owned privately or publicly). The issues at stake here became very clear to me during a panel discussion I took part in at one university. One of the audience of researchers asked whether different publishers had different cultures and, if so, whether this should influence the author's decision over which one to approach.

One member of the panel, a well-established professor who presented herself as a bastion of traditional academic values, was adamant in her response. The question of culture, she was sure, was a red herring. Commercial presses cared only about making a profit – that was all there was to be said about them. It was, therefore, crucial to be published by a university press, since such a press, freed from the constraints of profit maximisation, would devote more care to the quality of their publishing.

I was struck by this argument because it seemed to crystallise a widely held set of beliefs. Let us call this argument 'the Argument from Provenance'. This argument seems to me simplistic and one-sided. In my experience, the best commercial presses, such as Sage and Routledge, devote a good deal of attention to academic quality. They do so not out of altruism – though, as individuals, many of their staff are sympathetic to academic values – but precisely because the value of their brands depends on it. A commercial press publishing in academic markets without a reputation for quality has little value of any kind. It is, therefore, precisely because of the profit motive that commercial presses are concerned with quality.

University presses, meanwhile, most certainly do have to concern themselves with lucre. A university press that cavalierly disregarded the financial side of publishing would need always to be subsidised by its parent university. In the modern world, most universities are both unable and unwilling to provide such subsidies and some may expect a press to make a positive contribution to university finances. No university is prepared simply to hand its press a blank cheque.

As a result, university presses, when they are commissioning books, do much the same kinds of things as commercial presses. They estimate sales quantities and the impact of discounts; they budget for production costs; and they seek to use price to bring the various figures into an acceptable ratio.

To see how these issues play out in practice, let's consider as an example Edinburgh University Press. At the time of writing, the most recent accounts available are those dated July 2007. The professor mentioned above would no doubt note with approval that the press is a registered charity, almost wholly owned by its parent university, and that the trustees note in the preamble to the accounts that the press's objectives include education, 'the advancement of knowledge' and (a wonderful phrase straight from the Scottish Enlightenment) 'scholarly … utility'. The trustees also note that the press's 'publishing is recognized as being of the highest quality as monitored by the University's Press Committee which has to approve all titles proposed for publication' – a claim that perhaps the professor and I could agree over. I cannot help noticing, however, that from a financial point of view the press seems to have been neither carefree nor careless. Total incoming resources for the year in question amounted to £2,075,895 whilst total resources expended amounted to £2,064,693. That is, the press made a small profit.

The trustees' key objectives for the next year might, I suspect, surprise the professor a little. They were to: grow top-line sales; increase overall gross margin; increase operating profit; launch a new online journals system; improve the press's website and its use of its database; and implement a new business plan for journals. The language of the trustees seems to me just a tad commercial. This should come as no surprise: university presses, after all, exist in the real world.

Now let's consider briefly an academic press from the other side of the (supposed) fence. Polity Press is a privately owned company. At the time of writing it has, according to the company's latest return, three shareholders. Though small (the latest accounts report assets of less than £2 million), the company is a multinational (well, it has offices in the UK and USA). Its sales and distribution are in the hands of WileyBlackwell, a large multinational conglomerate.

According to the Argument from Provenance, we should be gravely suspicious of this nakedly capitalist press. Yet Polity's three shareholders happen to be: David Held, Professor of Political Science at the London School of Economics (LSE); Anthony Giddens, former Director of the LSE; and John Thompson, Professor of Sociology at the University of Cambridge. Professors Thompson and Held are also directors of Polity, as until recently was Professor Giddens. Do these gentlemen, when they leave their studies and enter Polity's offices, really leave behind all regard for academic standards? The company's publishing programme, which includes such academic luminaries as

Clifford Geertz, Zygmunt Baumann, and Jurgen Habermas, would seem to indicate the opposite.

In short, the dichotomy supposed to exist between, on the one hand, the unworldly presses of universities and learned societies, motivated purely by a Platonic love of truth and blissfully unconcerned with finance, and, on the other, capitalist presses corrupted by a lust for profit and blind to academic values is, I suggest, a myth. The Argument from Provenance does not correspond to objective differences between sectors.

Publishing does not, however, consist purely of objective processes. Subjective beliefs also play a role. And here I would concede that there is a point to what the good professor had to say. For within academia, university presses do, in general, enjoy greater prestige than do their commercial counterparts. The difference in the academic prestige accorded to the two sectors may be founded on mythical beliefs about how the two sectors operate, but is real nonetheless. It does not, however, necessarily follow that all university presses enjoy high prestige or that no commercial presses do: prestige depends on more than just the Argument from Provenance.

To see how these two variables that we have considered – size and provenance – play out together in practice, let us consider briefly the experience of an academic organisation that I came across a little while ago. The organisation used to compile a series of books, consisting of one edited book each year. They had been published by a large university press and the organisation had been pleased with the sales figures. Evidently they had reaped the benefits of economies of scale, especially in the form of export sales. But the press had then reorganised and the series had ended up on a different list with a commissioning editor who seemed less familiar with the type of book in question. Here we see an example of the danger of being a small fish in a large pond.

The academics decided it might be beneficial to change publishers and so approached a number of smaller publishers, each of whom were close to the market the series was targeted at. Each responded positively, sensing that the series had potential. Here we see the advantage of working with niche players. In the end, the offer that the academics accepted was one from a university press. They felt, perhaps rightly, that the university press in question enjoyed greater academic prestige than its commercial competitors and that this would help attract contributors to the series. But the final decision was not arrived at easily, because the academics had been impressed by the sympathy for the series displayed by some of the commissioning editors from the commercial presses they had approached – precisely the kind of thing that, according to the Argument from Provenance in its pure form, is not supposed to happen.

This story seems to me entirely unremarkable. It is the kind of thing that is going on in academic publishing all the time. What does it demonstrate? First, that it helps to take one's bearings, to know where in the publishing landscape one finds oneself and how the land lies. And, second, that there is more than one way to navigate that landscape, that different routes each have their own advantages, and indeed that the options need first to be explored and then to be kept under review.

CHANGES IN THE LANDSCAPE

The first half of this chapter sought to provide a view of the landscape of academic publishing as it is configured currently. But if we look more closely, we will see that changes are afoot. The purpose of the second half of this chapter is to identify these changes and, tentatively, to look ahead to see what effects they might have.

We will begin with the structure of the industry. In the publishing industry, corporate activity, in the form of mergers and acquisitions, is endemic. In particular, large companies are forever taking over smaller ones. There are many reasons for such activity, of which the main driver is simply the existence of the type of economies of scale outlined above.

Many academic authors have experienced at first hand the changes that result from corporate activity. An author might sign a contract with one publishing house and think that, as a result, they know where they stand, only to find that their publishers promptly (and without warning) get taken over by another. The imprint on the author's book might not be the one they originally expected. The team of people working on the book might also have changed. And (for better or worse) there is, of course, no guarantee that the process will stop there: the acquiring company might in turn be acquired by a bigger fish. Take, for instance, the example of the education studies market. In the UK one of the most important publishers in this field was Falmer Press. Falmer was taken over by Routledge. Authors under contract to Falmer began to find their books being published under a new imprint, called RoutledgeFalmer. And, as noted above, Routledge was in due course acquired by Taylor & Francis, who were in turn acquired by Informa.

Now consider the situation of an education studies author who had decided to publish not with Falmer but with, say, David Fulton or Kogan Page. Kogan Page sold its education list to Routledge. David Fulton, meanwhile, was acquired by Granada, which in due course sold it on to ... well, strangely enough, to Routledge.

It is entirely understandable that authors who have experienced corporate activity of this type often conclude that small publishing companies are disappearing from the scene, and that academic publishing will soon be entirely in the hands of a few vast multinational conglomerates.

Understandable, but mistaken. The problem with the view that publishing will become entirely oligopolistic is that it ignores one key feature of publishing economics. For, just as one end of the spectrum is characterised by economies of scale, so the other end is characterised by low barriers to entry. That is, it is possible to establish a new publishing company without a great deal of capital. As a result, new small publishers are being founded all the time, so that, as one generation of minnows get taken over, so another generation takes their place. This is a cycle that is likely to continue, because it seems to suit everyone involved. It allows large companies to focus on their core processes and, in effect, to outsource research and development of new markets to nimbler, more speculative, smaller companies. Then, when one of those companies succeeds in growing a profitable list, the larger company acquires it – often providing the owners of the smaller company with a welcome payout.

The moral of this story is that, paradoxically, as an academic author you need to remain vigilant, yet you can relax. You need to remain vigilant because the landscape is forever changing as some companies get taken over whilst new ones are founded. It is particularly important to keep an eye on the young companies in your field, some of which might provide new opportunities to publish. At the same time, you can relax, because the two key economic facts of the industry – economies of scale, but low barriers of entry – make it likely that the pattern of corporate activity will reproduce itself, leaving the structure of the industry rather more stable than one might expect.

The second change we should examine is the reorganisation of the monograph market. Changes in this market have been much discussed. Most commentators, however, have preferred to talk of its 'demise' or 'death', rather than mere reorganisation. In the academic and publishing press, laments for the genre appear on a regular basis. Susan Bassnett explained in an article in the *Times Higher Educational Supplement* that:

> Once, not so long ago, a postgraduate could expect to publish a good doctoral thesis, but today you have to advise your students to forget about a book and aim instead at a few articles. As for conference proceedings, which have never sold well in the UK, the prospect of finding anyone willing to publish even a stellar collection of essays is probably zero.

In *Books in the Digital Age*, John Thompson, whom we met above, has helpfully synthesised the data for the monograph market. He shows that, over the decades, the average number of copies sold per title has tended to decline. The reason is in part that library budgets have increasingly been consumed by competing products, notably journals and electronic products. Data of this sort provide some evidence for the view that the monograph market is, at best, on its last legs.

Yet, as indeed Thompson helps to show, one of the reasons that sales quantities per title have tended to decline is that monographs have taken sales from each other. There are more academic authors and more academic publishing than there used to be. A crowded market is not normally an indication of a moribund genre. Moreover, some of the electronic products that have stolen a share of library budgets are in fact monographs, in the guise of e-books.

I talk of a reorganisation, rather than the death, of the monograph market because the publishing industry has learnt to accommodate these changes. The twin processes of globalisation and technological change – a monograph written and published in the West may now, for example, be copy-edited in India and printed in China – have enabled publishers to cut their cloth more economically. They have also found that the library market can bear higher prices. Monograph prices today are high in comparison to consumer publishing, but competitive when compared (more relevantly) to journal subscriptions.

As a result, many publishers now in fact see the monograph market as a growth opportunity. In particular, whenever large publishers divert resources away from the monograph market, smaller publishers rush in to take their place. Consider, for example, the following announcement on the website of I. B. Tauris, an independent social science publisher:

Tauris Academic Studies is a new peer-reviewed academic imprint from I. B. Tauris, established for the publication of scholarly monographs and other original research, including work deriving from a doctoral thesis or dissertation.

With the 'Death of the Monograph' crisis that has swept the academic and publishing worlds in recent years, a consensus has emerged that the scholarly monograph, the specifically focused treatise that is at the heart of academic publishing, is an endangered species. *Tauris Academic Studies* is designed to alleviate this problem.

According to this announcement, the series publishes about 100 titles per year. This illustrates the increasing role played in monograph publishing by the more entrepreneurial independent presses. It illustrates too that reports of the death of the monograph are greatly exaggerated.

The third and final development in academic publishing that we should consider is the impact of digital technology. To date, digital technology has proved to be a benevolent force in the publishing industry. Books are well suited to Internet retailing. Amazon was one of the first online retailers to establish a brand – a fact that helped to increase the availability of books and, I suggest, to refresh their image. Yet because it has taken a long time to develop highly readable screen technology, questions of digital rights management and piracy have been less pressing than in the music industry.

Three recent or current developments deserve particular attention. The first is the development of digital pre-press processes. Journal publishers were quick off the mark to develop paperless, web-based, authoring and editing systems that allowed a number of users – peer reviewers, for example – instant access to text at various stages of developments. Such systems are now being marketed to book publishers, enabling them to reduce the time and cost of editorial and production processes. Such practices as shifting typescripts or proofs around by disc, e-mail attachment, or courier remain widespread, but are beginning to feel clunky and dated.

A second technological trend is the development of high-quality digital printing, which is steadily replacing litho-printing in the industry. The quality of digital publishing has now improved to the point where most readers cannot discern a difference from litho-printed books. Litho-printing involves set-up costs, which tends to make small print runs unprofitable. Digital printing, in contrast, is much better suited to small print runs. This reduces the amount of capital that publishers need to tie up in stocks, makes it more cost-effective to keep backlist titles in print even when their rate of sales has declined, and makes niche publishing more viable.

Digital printing even enables print-on-demand (PoD) publishing, where publishers can keep a title 'in print' (i.e. available on their list) without stock: copies may be printed to meet particular orders – even, in extreme cases, orders for single copies. PoD also makes self-publishing more affordable.

A third trend is the improvement in the readability of text on screens, notably through the replacement of backlit liquid crystal display systems with electronic ink. The latest generation of dedicated e-readers are, it has been widely agreed, as kind on the eyes as paper. These are being supplemented by larger screen devices, designed primarily for the reading of documents (such as contracts) but also suitable for reading e-books from. This has changed the terms of the debate over the merits of print and electronic display. The pertinent question is no longer 'Why would you want to read a book from a screen, when it is so much less readable than paper?', but rather, 'What is the point of paper?'

The week before I drafted this chapter, in late 2008, I found myself at a dinner, sitting next to a representative of the paper industry. The conversation turned to Plastic Logic's flexible electronic reading technology, slated for commercial release in 2009. 'Do you think this really will be the death of print?' I asked him.

'Yes', he said.

So do I. A few years ago, I had to leave my suit behind in a hotel room in New York. I had bought some books in Barnes & Noble and there wasn't room in my suitcase for both them and the suit. There were e-book reading devices around in those days too, but only geeks used them. Next time I go to New York, I won't have to throw away any suits.

What are the implications of technological change for academic authorship? In such a dynamic environment, it would be unwise to make a detailed prophecy. Indeed, I do not know anyone genuinely in a position to do so. It is possible, however, to venture some broad-brush suggestions. Mine are as follows:

1. Technological invention is one thing, commercial exploitation another. The publishing industry will change, as it always has done, in response to technological development – but business models will change less quickly than the underlying technology.
2. In particular, although technology has already reached a stage where it is possible to envisage the end of paper, I doubt that paper publishing will disappear overnight. In academic publishing, e-books have to date tended to replace hardback publications (reference books and monographs) more than softback. In consumer publishing, it may happen the other way around. Anthony Cheetham, who is Chairman of Quercus Publishing and perhaps the nearest thing the industry has to a genuine prophet, has suggested that there may be a mixed economy, in which e-books substitute for paperbacks (both are portable and disposable, but e-books have advantages such as searchability) whilst hardbacks survive to satisfy consumers' bibliophile instincts.
3. In any case, the issue of paper versus e-ink, whilst important for booksellers and printers, is of secondary importance for authors. Of greater importance to them is the use of technology in pre-publication processes. Here, production cycles are likely to accelerate and the gap between writing and publishing to shorten. Authorship is also likely to become a more collaborative process as open-access software (wikis and web-hosted editorial management systems) make it easier for editors, reviewers, readers, and so on to contribute throughout a project. As a result, writing a book will feel more like making a radio or television programme.
4. The function of publishers will change. At present, most publishers fulfil two functions simultaneously: they co-ordinate publishing

services (copy-editing, typesetting, design, and so on) and they brand products. There is no reason why these two functions need always to be fulfilled by the same organisation. As access to the technology of publishing broadens, so organisations with quality brands in academia – learned societies, research institutes, and universities – are likely to seek to provide the branding themselves and outsource the co-ordination function to publishing services firms (providing book-packaging, distribution, and so on).

Overall, it is difficult to see how or why the development of faster, smarter, less expensive technology should lead to anything other than a burgeoning of opportunity for academic authors.

The spirit of this book is based on a conviction (regarded by some as heretical) that we already live in a golden age for academic authorship – and it is possible that there is a platinum age to come.

SUMMARY

1. Get your bearings. Get to know the lie of the land. In particular, map publishing companies according to their size and provenance.
2. Decide whether you would rather be a big fish in a small pond or a small fish in a big pond.
3. Keep an eye on changes in academic publishing. In particular, observe the development of small, entrepreneurial, companies in the niches in which you are interested. Watch too for the extension into publishing of quality brands from other parts of academia.

CHAPTER 3

Getting commissioned

There are two ways of getting commissioned. You may have an idea and propose it to a publisher, who may then offer you a contract in return. Or an editor may have an idea for a book and then ask you to write it. We can call the first 'reactive' commissioning (reactive on the part of the editor, that is) and the second, 'proactive'. The bulk of this chapter will be about the former, but first let's look briefly at how you can increase the likelihood of an editor approaching you with an invitation to write a book.

PROACTIVE COMMISSIONING

There are many reasons why editors devise ideas for books. They are close to the market and receive many suggestions and requests ('Why don't you publish a book on …?'; 'Are you publishing anything on …?'). They watch their competitors, looking to imitate their most successful books or fill any gaps left in the market. They seek to make their own lists more coherent and consistent. They have annual commissioning targets that cannot always be met by relying on the flow of proposals from authors. And many editors are creative people in their own right and enjoy producing ideas for projects.

Many authors doubt that there is anything they can do to influence this process. If an idea for a book originates with the editor, who then decides whom to approach to write it, isn't this all in the hands of the editor? This, apparently, is the assumption of the standard guides available to academic authors, all of which simply pass over the business of proactive commissioning. It is, however, wrong.

Every editor I know makes use of 'soft' information. Editors make use of chance encounters, overheard comments, and odd coincidences. They rely to an extraordinary extent on networking. There are times when it feels to me as if networking is *all* there is to the job! It follows that, if – to use a metaphor that editors themselves sometimes use – you can get your name onto their radar, the chances at some point of being invited to write a book are very much greater.

The people who show up most on editors' radar are those who have already published. This may sound like a 'Catch 22': if you want to get commissioned, you need to have published, but in order to get published, you need to have been commissioned. There is, however, no need to feel dispirited. 'Getting published', after all, covers a range of possibilities.

It is helpful here to think of a ladder of authorship. No form of writing – including non-academic writing – is too modest to serve as the first rung on the ladder. A good place to start, indeed, is on the correspondence pages of newspapers. I am not the only editor to scan these as much to see who is writing as what they are writing about. I once read in the *Financial Times* a letter about higher education. I contacted John Fazey, one of the letter's authors, at the University of Wales in order to find about more about the views that he had expressed in the letter. I ended up commissioning him to edit a series. John told me when I met him that writing letters to the press was part of his team's strategy to generate interest in their research.

Publishing articles in magazines or on the Internet is a particularly effective way of getting noticed. They signal to editors not only that you are active in a certain field but also that you can and do write. I recently recommended a social scientist to an editor whom I knew to be looking for an author to write a book, aimed at the consumer market, on a particular social issue. The author had written some articles on *spiked*, an issues-based website. 'Oh, yes', said the editor, 'he writes on *spiked*'. Note that word, 'Yes'!

Another rung on the ladder is provided by the opportunity to write grey literature. Grey literature consists of all forms of documents – reports, discussion papers, pamphlets, and so on – that are 'published' in the original sense of the word (i.e. 'made public'), but not necessarily with all the hallmarks of formal publication – such as bindings, spines, ISBNs, or prices. Grey literature used to be very ephemeral. Now, thanks in part to improved methods of librarianship and, especially, search engines on the Internet, grey literature remains visible (and so can show up on editors' radar) for longer.

Consider one example of the efficacy of grey literature. One author I have worked with – Spinder Dhaliwal – published in 1998 an A5, stapled, booklet about Asian entrepreneurship called *Silent Contributors*. It is still referenced on the Internet. The booklet has helped to build Spinder's reputation in the subject and demonstrated her ability to write well. She has since gone on to write a book on Asian entrepreneurship called *Making a Fortune*, published by John Wiley.

The metaphor of the ladder of authorship is not, of course, entirely precise. Not every author starts by writing letters to the press and dutifully works upwards one rung at a time, through the writing of articles, grey literature, and so on. But the metaphor does have one great advantage: it demonstrates that the best way to get commissioned is to start writing, now.

So far I have said nothing about articles in scholarly journals. I hesitate to include them on the ladder of authorship leading to the writing of books. Such articles can, after all, be even more difficult to get published – and, in some ways, in academia they can count for more. More fundamentally, I have not found the link between the writing of journal articles and of books to be very strong. One might expect, for example, that in companies that publish both journals and books, editors of the former would alert editors of the latter to articles that might form the basis of subsequent books. In practice, however, the editors usually work in different offices and each have their own preoccupations, so such communication is rare. I have tried to remedy this in my work as an editor by wading though dozens of back copies of journals in order to find arresting articles and then contacting the authors to discuss the idea of writing a book – but I have only rarely succeeded in commissioning a book in this way. For whatever reason, the authorial link between journal articles and books seems weaker than that between books and many less academic forms of writing.

There are, of course, other ways to network besides writing. Many of the simplest ways are the best. Carry your business card with you, always. Attach your contact details to any piece of writing, routinely. Remember the power of the positive: if you enjoy an article, paper, or presentation, write to the author concerned to say so. (Strangely enough, most people enjoy telling other people about their fans more than their critics.) Public speaking – not only giving papers at academic conferences, but also talks, presentations, panel discussions, and so on – are also effective networking activities. Again, the Internet amplifies the effect.

The Internet may provide the means by which an editor first discovers you or be the place to which an editor who has already heard your name goes in order to discover more about you. The best way to capitalise on this is to have your own web space, even if it is only a page. If you doubt the need for this, try Googling yourself. You may well find that the portrait that emerges is a rather arbitrary one in which the qualities that are most likely to attract editors are drowned in a sea of such inconsequential details as your time in the local half-marathon three years ago. Having your own web space enables you to provide a more focused portrait. It need be neither extensive nor elaborate, so long as it is clear, accurate, and up to date. I am always surprised at how few academics make good use of the Internet's networking potential.

Overall, proactive commissioning is a major form of editorial activity. The good news here is that an editor who has a good idea for a book, but no author to write it, has a problem to which you may be the solution. The art of networking is, of course, far from precise. You cannot be entirely sure whose radar you end up on or which projects this will be in connection with. But as an editor I am certain that, by some strange process of osmosis (perhaps 'karma' would be a better word), prospective authors who are organised and energetic about networking do, one way or another, reap rewards.

REACTIVE COMMISSIONING

The standard way in which academic authors get commissioned is by sending a proposal to an editor. The first task here is to decide which publishers to approach. Unfortunately, authors often waste their efforts by sending proposals to publishers that simply are not appropriate for the books they have in mind. Such proposals go into the waste bin unread.

I suspect that many authors make this mistake because they see publishers simply as devices for transforming typescripts into finished books. If indeed the work of publishers consisted only of the processes of physical transformation (principally, copy-editing, type-setting, proofreading, designing, printing, and binding), it might not matter very much which publishers authors sent their proposals to. Such a conception, however, ignores three crucial aspects of the publishing industry:

1. Each company is a bundle of contractual relationships – with suppliers, distributors, representatives, wholesalers, retailers, export agents, investors, banks, and so on.
2. Each company has its own corporate personality. Companies differ from each other in their histories, in what they know or understand, and in what they like or feel at home with.
3. As we saw above (pp. 16–17), the economics of publishing depends on economies of scale. A company that has, say, published 100 books in a subject is likely to publish the 101st book efficiently. It will know, for example, which colleges offer courses in the subject, which periodicals will want review copies, and which retailers will be key. It will already have sections in its catalogue and on its website in which the book may be promoted. For the publisher, therefore, slotting in the 101st book on a subject will prove more economical than publishing a first title in some other field.

Some, at least, of these concerns will seem distant or even be hidden from authors. How many authors, for example, either know or care about their publishers' contracts with their distributors? Yet each of these aspects impacts on such matters as the quality of a company's publishing, the markets that company can reach, and so on. In combination they account for the fundamentally important fact that each publishing house will be better suited to some types of books than others.

To see how this plays out in practice, consider the example of an author who, say, wishes to publish a book on research methods in Tourism Studies. For this book we can ignore the non-academic presses: this is a book written by an academic on an academic subject for academic readers. For this author, academic publishers will divide into two main categories: those that do not publish in this area and would not be suitable for such a book; and those that have a list in the subject. (There is also perhaps a grey area, consisting of companies that publish some titles in this area without having a complete list in the subject.)

Those publishers that *do* have a list in this area themselves divide into different types. For the sake of simplicity, let us say there are three such presses. Press A perhaps belongs to a university or professional body. It might publish such a book if it were suitable as a monograph to be read by experts and researchers. Press B might be an international conglomerate that might publish the book if it were suitable for use as a student text. Press C, an independent press, might fit somewhere in between the two. It might consider the book as something in between a monograph and a student text – as, say, a subsidiary or upper-level text.

Now there will be important differences between these presses' publishing strategies. Press A might publish in hardback at a high price and with a low print run. Press B would publish in paper with a lower price and much higher run. And Press C would choose an intermediate strategy, perhaps publishing first in hardback and then in paper (though not at a low price). Sales figures too would vary between presses in terms of their totals, their geographical distribution, and their rhythm over time.

Clearly, then, the author's decision over which publishers to approach is important. On this will depend such questions as whether the book will get published, how it will be published, which readers will buy it, and whether it will prove successful.

Selecting your publisher

In order to distinguish between companies, it will help to build up a mental map of academic publishing. Broadly, there are three types of publisher in this field:

1. There are general academic publishers that publish in several genres and across a wide range of subjects. Most of these companies are large. They include, for example, WileyBlackwell, Routledge (now part of Informa), Princeton University Press, and the publisher of this book. There are, however, also some smaller companies in this category – Edinburgh University Press or Boydell & Brewer, for example.

2. There are publishers that specialise by subject. They publish across a narrow range of subjects, though they may publish in several genres. Companies such as Eerdmans (theology), Human Kinetics (sport), Multilingual Matters (applied linguistics), and The Policy Press (social policy) belong to this category.

3. There are publishers that specialise by genre. For example, ABC-CLIO, Four Courts Press, and Learning Matters specialise in reference books, monographs, and textbooks respectively.

As you research potential publishers for your book, this taxonomy will help make sense of the publishing strategies of different companies and make them easier to remember.

I suggest using a three-stage approach to selecting publishers. The first stage is to generate a long list of potential publishers. It is important at this point to be as exhaustive as possible. Begin by noting the publishers of those books on your own shelves which most resemble the book that you want to write. Use your colleagues to add to this list. Listen to what they say – they may have useful 'soft' information based on their own experience and contacts – but pay at least as much attention to the 'hard' evidence provided by the books sitting on their shelves: when all is said and done, that tells you which publishers' products they rate highly enough to actually spend money on. Visit your campus bookstore and library and note the publishers of books on the particular shelves that you wish your work to end up on. Next add the names of publishers who exhibit at relevant conferences or have their books reviewed in relevant journals. Add too the names of publishers culled from reading lists (either recommended reading lists for courses or notes on further reading in books). Finally, use databases to ensure you've left no stone unturned. Here online retailers are a rich source of information. I find it particularly useful to search for a comparable book on Amazon and then follow the links to other books provided under the heading 'Customers who bought this book also bought'.

By the time you have completed the first stage of the process, you should feel confident that you have 'captured' the appropriate publishers for your book. Their name will be lurking somewhere in the list now in front of you. The second stage is to refine your list. Work through each name on your list, asking yourself whether you can see any specific reason why that company might be suitable publishers. Use companies' websites or catalogues to check that they are still publishing in your area. Remember, there is no use trying to fit square pegs into round holes. If you cannot see any reason why some particular company might publish your book, delete it from your list.

You now have your hit list. The third and final stage of this process is to prioritise the names on the list. You can do this diagrammatically by setting out your list in the form of three concentric circles. Consider each company carefully, asking yourself how strong the evidence is that it publishes (a) in your subject, (b) in the appropriate genre, and (c) at the appropriate level. Place the names of the strongest candidates in the centre circle and those of the fringe candidates in the outer. If a company publishes an actual series into which your book could happily be slotted, this may well be a case of 'Bull's-eye!'

Making your pitch

The standard way of pitching to publishers is by sending a formal written proposal. There is little variation between publishers in the type of information they require. The following specification, taken from Cambridge University Press's website, is typical:

---

1. Title
2. Reasons for writing, proposed length and amount of illustration
3. Intended completion date
4. General overall account of content of book, list of chapters and indication of content of each chapter
5. Brief credentials of author(s)
6. Level of presentation
7. The readership and market for the book
8. Comparison with competing books.

However, the *form* in which publishers require such information does vary. Some publishers like to receive proposals electronically, others prefer hard copy, while some are happy with either. Many publishers have designed their own pro formas for book proposals. Appendix A provides a set of proposal guidelines that I developed as a commissioning editor. Other examples are downloadable from company websites. If a company has its own pro forma, be sure to use it. Resist any temptation to send your proposal in some other form whilst thinking, 'Well, the information's all in there somewhere, I'm sure the editor will be able to extract the information required.' If you depart from the publishers' preferred form, you will make it more difficult for the editor to feed your proposal into the company's internal database – and signal that you are an unco-operative author.

Many first-time authors find book proposals difficult to write. This is not surprising, given that many have never read anyone else's book proposals. To see why this makes the task difficult, one has only to imagine what it would be like trying to write, say, a journal article if one had never seen an academic journal. We all learn from models. If any of your colleagues have had book proposals accepted by publishers, it may well be worth asking whether you could read the proposal. In addition, Appendix B provides, by way of example, the proposal that I wrote for this book. (I don't pretend that it's perfect, but at least it was successful.)

In my experience, there are three aspects of book proposals on which authors often require guidance, namely the provision of information about (a) the market for the book, (b) the reason why people will buy the book, and (c) competing titles. It is important to recognise that the purpose of your pitch is not only to outline the contents of the book and its intellectual rationale, but also, in effect, to provide a mini-business plan to persuade publishers to invest several thousand dollars in your project.

Let's consider the question of the market first. In order to commission your book, an editor will need to propose it to a publishing meeting at which colleagues from other departments, including sales and marketing, are present. At some point in the discussion – probably quite early on – the question 'Who is going to buy this book?' will arise. Sometimes the editor will actually begin the discussion with this information by saying, for example, 'This is aimed at scholars and researchers specialising in the Old Testament' or 'This book will be read by undergraduates in the second or third year of a Linguistics course.'

You need to ensure that your proposal provides the editor with the equivalent sentence for your book. When doing so, be both rigorous and precise. Editors often come across sentences such as the following (to take a putative textbook on Communication Studies as an example): 'This book will be of interest to undergraduates, postgraduates, scholars and researchers, public relations officers (PROs), journalists, executives, politicians, policy-makers, and the general reader.' How likely is it really that a book sufficiently advanced to appeal to scholars or practical enough for PROs will also interest the general public? If, when you are trying to define the market for your book, you find yourself yoking together a long list of increasingly disparate groups, that is probably a sign that you need to think the book through more rigorously. If in doubt, experiment by writing a passage of the text itself. Usually a few sentences will be sufficient to show that the text cannot be all things to all people. The decisions you will find yourself having to make over such matters as tone, style, and vocabulary in order to appeal to one group of readers will in effect tend to exclude at least some other groups of readers.

Books do, of course, sometimes appeal to more than one group of readers. Usually, however, these groups will not be of equal importance. Where this is the case, it is helpful to distinguish between the main and subsidiary markets. Take (to turn to an actual example) *Using Communication Theory* by Sven Windahl *et al.* This book deals not only with pure communication theory, but also with questions of application involving such issues as organisational theory and the processes of innovation and diffusion. A search on Google indicates that, as well as being used by its target market, namely undergraduate and postgraduate courses in Communication Studies, the book is also used in business schools on management and economics courses. In a proposal for such a book, therefore, one might provide something along the lines of the following: 'The main market for this book is on higher education courses in Communication Studies. This includes both undergraduate and postgraduate students. In addition, because the book deals with issues of organisational and consumer behaviour, there is a subsidiary market on management and economics courses in business schools.' This is both more rigorous and more precise (and truthful too!).

When trying to define the market for your book, you may be tempted to use a construction such as 'This book will appeal to all those readers interested in X' (where 'X' is the subject of the book).

Avoid this temptation. The problem with such constructions is that they hinge on the word 'interest'. Interest is a very thin thing. Though we may out of interest read an article in a newspaper, say, or visit a website, this motive is rarely strong enough to make us buy academic books. Before buying such a book, customers will usually need to believe that it will benefit them in some way.

For example, the book you are reading now will be 'of interest' to several types of people. I imagine that reviews of this book will be read by, for instance, other academic editors and by linguisticians who specialise in the study of academic discourse. But if you are reading this now, the chances are that you will belong to the group of people who (I trust!) stand most to benefit from it, namely actual or prospective academic authors. When writing your book proposal, therefore, ask yourself not 'Who will this be of interest to?' but rather 'Who needs this book? Who will it help? Who will *benefit* from it?'

You can extend the market for your book by maximising its export potential. In many Anglophone countries the domestic market is not large enough on its own to provide academic publishers with the sales they require to make a book profitable. Publishers need, therefore, to look for ways to sell the book abroad (directly by exporting copies and indirectly by selling territorial or translation rights to foreign publishers). The main exception to this rule is the United States, where the domestic market is large. Nevertheless, if you work in America it is still well worth considering how to boost your book's export potential. In particular, there is immediately to the north of the USA another populous, prosperous, book-buying nation.

There are several ways in which you can enhance the exportability of an academic book. You may, for example, provide examples or case studies from abroad, quote foreign experts, and cite foreign publications. You may assist foreign readers by including in your book a glossary of the culture-specific terms and acronyms that feature in your text. Even cosmetic measures – such as a foreword or endorsement from an expert in another country – will help to make your book exportable and hence more attractive to publishers.

You can also extend the market for your book by maximising its potential for sales over time. Avoid any temptation to rely purely on novel or topical points to sell your proposal. Fashions come and go in academia and the effect is to make some books perishable. Publishers do not want to be left with unsaleable stock in their warehouses. However novel or topical your book may be, show also how it relates to long-established or even perennial themes.

It may help at this stage to look back at the proposal in Appendix B, putting yourself in the shoes of a commissioning editor. How well does this proposal define its market? How clearly does it identify the benefits that the proposed book will provide to its readers? How well does it deal with the issues of exportability and perishability?

Finally, a word about competition. Publishers routinely ask prospective authors for information about competing titles. No question divides authors from publishers as clearly as this. Authors will often assume that a lack of competition for their books is a good sign and that editors' entrepreneurial appetites will be whetted by reading in a proposal that 'there is no other book on this subject'. Some authors even suppress information about competing texts in order to present the proposed book as unique.

In fact, however, uniqueness makes publishers jittery. They tend to assume that if there is no book on a subject, that is because there is no market for one. There is a saying amongst publishers that 'if there are twenty books on a subject, you should publish the twenty-first'. Be sure, therefore, to give plentiful information about titles that your book will compete against. Once you have done so, you may then identify what is distinctive and advantageous about the book you are proposing to write. Avoid any temptation to exaggerate the defects or deny the merits of books already published, since to do so risks making you appear imperceptive or untrustworthy. If there really isn't any competition for your book, seek to suggest reasons why – other than that the market is too small!

SUMMARY

1. Authors win commissions either by being invited to write books or by pitching to publishers.
2. You may boost your chances of the former by networking effectively and by beginning to climb the 'ladder of authorship'.
3. Before sending a book proposal, research the market and select the most appropriate publishers.
4. Ensure your proposal is in the publishers' preferred form.

5. Define the market for your book rigorously and precisely.
6. Emphasise the benefits that your book will provide to its readers.
7. Enhance the exportability of your book.
8. Minimise the perishability of your book.
9. Analyse the titles in competition with your book.

CHAPTER 4

Contracts and agents

Let us say that, following Chapter 3, you have discussed your proposed book with a commissioning editor; the editor has responded favourably and formally proposed the project to the publishing company concerned; and now announces to you that the company has decided that it wishes to commission the book. What next?

CONTRACTS

The first step is to ensure you receive the contract as soon as possible. Though the issuing of author contracts is standard practice in the publishing industry, there can be a delay between the editor promising a contract and one being dispatched. Usually this creates no problem beyond irritation, but occasionally difficulties arise: details discussed in conversation become forgotten, for example; the editor moves to another post; or the list is acquired by another company. It's always best, therefore, to press for a contract as soon as possible.

Once you have received the contract, do read it. Though that might sound too obvious to need saying, I frequently come across cases of authors signing contracts without having read them. As an editor, few things annoy me more than asking an author to abide by the contract, only to find that the author has no knowledge of what is in the contract – and perhaps even implies that insistence on abiding by the contract is somehow ungentlemanly. Needless to say, arguing against a set of conditions one has put one's name to is not a strong position. The contract, then, does matter: it is an agreement between consenting adults, not merely some form of ritualistic handshake.

How, then, to read the contract? Contracts vary considerably between projects, between companies, and between territories.

Nevertheless, it is helpful to look at what might be called a typical contract. Even if your own contract differs from the model below, the latter is useful for comparative purposes. I should at this stage make clear that I am not a lawyer and neither is this book intended as a legal work. The account below, therefore, is informal and non-technical: it is intended as an introductory guide, rather than an authoritative statement. (For the latter, there is really no alternative to consulting a lawyer.)

Publishing contracts typically include six components. Using plain, as opposed to legal, language, we may examine these under the following headings:

1. The framework
2. Rights
3. The product
4. The process
5. Remuneration
6. Meta-text

The framework will specify the parties to the contract and a commencement date. These usually appear at or near the top of the contract. In addition, usually towards the bottom, there will be a statement about assignment, specifying under what circumstances the contract may be assigned to other parties.

The part(s) of the contract dealing with rights will typically cover both moral rights and copyright. Broadly, an author's moral rights include (a) the right to paternity (to be acknowledged as the originator of the text) and (b) the right to integrity (the right not to have the text abridged without consent). Copyright is a form of intellectual property. Typically, a publishing contract will state who owns the rights at the outset, which rights the author is granting to the publisher (under what conditions, and for how long), and whether and how these rights may revert to the author.

The clauses of the contract dealing with the product will specify: the extent of the work (usually in terms of thousands of words); its contents (especially the number of figures of various kinds to be included); and when and how the typescript will be delivered to the publishers. It might also include some specification of the intended publication format (for example, 'in hardback first') and date (for example, within 'eighteen months of delivery of the typescript to the publishers'). The contract will certainly require the author to make a number of warranties about the work – for example, that it is indeed the author's own work and that it is not in any way unlawful (for example, through being libellous). In addition, it will specify that, in the case of a breach of such warranties, the author will indemnify the publishers against any loss or damage that results.

Clauses dealing with the publishing process will contain specifications of who is going to do what, when. For example, how soon after they have received the typescript, and by what criteria, will the publishers decide whether the typescript is acceptable. Statements about who will be responsible for the copy-editing, proofreading, and indexing are also likely to be included. In addition, there will be a statement about the control of publishing decisions: who, for example, will have the final say over such matters as the cover design or the type of paper used? (Usually the publishers will insist on having control over such decisions.)

As we have seen above (see pp. 4–5), a variety of arrangements for remuneration of authors is used. The clauses on remuneration will specify who is going to pay whom, when, and how payment will be made; and on what basis.

Finally, the contract will include 'meta-text' – that is, clauses about the contract itself. This will include, for example, specification of which country's laws will govern the contract and how, and under what circumstances, the contract may be terminated.

When you read the contract, do be sure to read every word. Subject the contract to two different kinds of readings. First, read it clause by clause: consider each clause in its own right; check whether you understand it. Second, read it all through again, but this time focusing on how the contract hangs together as a whole. Often one finds that the full significance of one clause willl depend on how it relates to other clauses in the same contract. As Carole Blake says, in *From Pitch To Publication*, 'contract clauses are like pieces of a jigsaw: you only get the full picture when you have all the pieces together'. To give one example: one author I commissioned was concerned that the contract did not guarantee that the publishers would actually publish the work (indeed, it specified circumstances under which we might not do so); he was concerned that he might devote several years' work to the book, all to no purpose. I pointed out to him that we were paying him a sizeable advance against royalties on signature of contract and that, if we then pulled the book, we would have to write this off as a loss. Though this didn't provide a guarantee of publication, it certainly represented a pretty big incentive for the publisher not to cancel the book.

If, when you are reading the contract, you come across parts that you do not understand, make a note of them and ask your publishers to explain. Some authors fail to do this because they feel that the publishers are hardly to be trusted, since they are the other party in the contract. I understand this reasoning and I don't say that publishers' responses are necessarily trustworthy, though to my knowledge I have yet to experience any dishonest dealing of this type. In my experience, the greater risk is that the editor, who is unlikely to have a legal training, might inadvertently give inaccurate answers. But I cannot see what an author stands to lose simply by raising queries. Below, we will consider what other sources of advice may be available to the author.

NEGOTIATING THE CONTRACT

Once you have read the contract and clarified its meaning, begin to negotiate. Do not be put off by suggestions that this can't be done. Contracts are not tablets of stone, descended from heaven: and even if they were, they could be replaced. If your editor says something along the lines of 'It's our standard contract, I'm afraid I can't change it', take that to mean 'Getting the contract changed might be a bit awkward for me and I don't really want to have to, I'd rather you just signed it.' Always seek to negotiate. In my experience, the very attempt is likely to gain respect. The worst that can happen is that you gain nothing through negotiation – in which case you are no worse off than if you hadn't made the attempt. Usually, however, you can make some headway.

Bear in mind that changes are not always zero-sum. That is to say, some changes may be in all parties' interests. It is in everyone's interest, for example, for the date for delivery of the typescript to be realistic. Often one can use these 'win-win' changes as a way of establishing that the contract is indeed capable of revision.

What kinds of revisions is an author likely to require? Resist a temptation to try to change everything in the contract and to pretend that everything is important. It is better to think clearly about the relative importance to you of each issue. Ask yourself what really matters and what is trivial.

Let's consider what features of a contract an author may wish to check or to negotiate over. The list that follows is organised according to the six headings we used above to outline the structure of a publishing contract. Please note, however, that the list is by no means intended to be exhaustive.

1. The framework
   a) Check the commencement date (at which the agreement comes into operation). Note this is not necessarily the date at which the contract is issued.
   b) Check who are the parties to the contract and that this is accurately stated. For example, in the case of a publishing group, is the contract with the subsidiary company or the parent company? If as an author you are representing an organisation (for example, a learned society that is subsidising your book), is the contract with the organisation or with you? (Usually it will be with the author. If it isn't, the author will require a separate contract with the organisation.)
   c) If, as is likely, the publishers wish to be able to assign the contract (for example, in the event of a corporate acquisition), you might argue that your consent would be required (though you may be asked to commit not to withhold such consent 'unreasonably').
2. Rights
   a) Check that the contract guarantees that your moral rights will be respected and formally asserted in the publication itself. Contracts sometimes omit this point. If in fact the publisher is intending not to publish the text as an integral work (they wish to incorporate it within a larger reference work, for example), raising this issue here will help to clarify these plans.
   b) Seek a clear statement that you own the copyright in the first place. Seek too to retain ownership of the rights: that is, seek to restrict the agreement to a licence for the publishers to publish

the work, as opposed to an actual transfer of ownership. If there is a reason why the publisher wishes to purchase ownership of the rights, one might expect this concession on the part of the author to be rewarded by the rate of remuneration.

c) Provided you retain ownership of the copyright, seek a clear statement of the circumstances under which rights will revert to you. Many authors overlook the significance of this. At contract stage, when you are just setting out on the project, the question of what happens when the work goes out of print may seem too far off to matter. However, it is possible that, at some point in the future, you may wish to get the rights to a work back – perhaps you wish to get a new edition published, or reissue the work by publishing it yourself, or simply to use part of the text in some other publication (a collection of readings, say). Seek to make the circumstances of reversion unequivocal. If, for example, the clause uses a phrase such as 'when the work is out of print', seek to include a precise definition of that phrase (note that a book may be 'out of stock' without necessarily being 'out of print'). Try, if possible, to avoid the situation whereby rights for the work in print fail to revert to you because the publisher happens to have published an electronic edition: such editions may remain on the market at negligible cost to the publisher, without actually selling.

3. The product

a) Seek to define the extent of the work in terms of a range rather than a single number. If the contract uses a single number (say, '70,000 words'), this inevitably creates a grey area: nobody ever writes exactly 70,000 words, so how much below or above this figure can you go? It is better to have a range (for example, 65,000–75,000 words).

b) Clarify not only the number of figures but also the type (for example: Black-and-white photographs? Line drawings?).

c) Publishers are usually reluctant to specify a period within which a work will be published. They might say, for example, that though they would expect to publish a work within a year of receiving the typescript, they cannot guarantee this because, well, stuff happens (proofs go astray, people fall ill, and so on).

And, in fact, there is some truth in that. The solution may be to push the date out until the point at which the publishers feel it's unreasonable to resist.

d) Be careful to ensure that whatever you warrant to be true is indeed true. For example, you will be asked to warrant that nobody else owns copyright on the work. This may not in fact be the case. For example, if you are writing a textbook, you may wish to include some course materials you wrote a couple of years back. But did you write them all yourself – or did a colleague help you? If the latter, the colleague is likely to have a claim on the copyright. Be meticulous about such matters and seek to resolve them before you sign the contract.

4. The Process

Be very careful about the indemnities. They may result in hefty liabilities. If the publishers are sued, say because of libel or plagiarism, they are likely to seek to pass on the financial liability to the author. It is, of course, perfectly reasonable for publishers to ask authors not to write texts that infringe the law. If an author plagiarises another writer, why shouldn't the author be liable? But one can at least try to build in some safeguards. You may, for example, ask for the right to be informed about any charge made against the work. You may also seek the right to be consulted, both concerning any charge and over the appointment of lawyers. In one case when I was a publishing director I received an allegation of plagiarism, accompanied by a threat of litigation. We could have turned to a lawyer and sent the resulting bill to the author. Fortunately, we consulted the author first, who was able to demonstrate that no plagiarism had occurred. It is very easy for authors to ignore the indemnity clauses on the grounds that they'd never knowingly do anything illegal. Unfortunately, authors do sometimes break the law inadvertently. In particular, it is easier to plagiarise unintentionally than one might think. Publishers will expect a publishing contract to include indemnities (if any of my authors just refused to agree to indemnities, my suspicions would be aroused and I would walk away from the deal without signing the contract), but as an author you should certainly devote care and attention to the clause. Nobody wants to lose their home as a result of writing a book!

5. Remuneration
   a) Often, contract negotiations focus almost exclusively on remuneration. I am not sure this is sensible: the amounts at stake may be small and other points, such as those discussed above, may be more important. Besides which, in negotiations I would never want to focus exclusively on any one thing. Often the way one makes progress in negotiations is by discussing more than one clause at a time and then agreeing to trade concessions ('Look, if you were able to agree to my request on clause X, I could look again at your request on clause Y'). To reach such compromises, you need to be negotiating on more than one front.
   b) Often the key to progress over remuneration lies in a rising royalty. The publishers have offered you, let us say, a royalty of 5 per cent of net receipts. You want 10 per cent. The editor flatly refuses to budge. She says that the book is costly to produce, the market is price-sensitive, and so on, and her company simply doesn't have a margin to negotiate in. What do you do then? One solution is to try to ascertain what sales forecast the editor is working on. You can then suggest that, if the book does better than that, the publishers would have room for manoeuvre: they'd be making more money than they expected, so could afford to pay you more. You could propose, therefore, a 'rising' royalty (otherwise known as a 'stepped' royalty) whereby, once sales reach a certain threshold, the royalty rate rises. This is, I find, one of the easiest points to win in negotiation – mainly because the principle is fair and reasonable. It enables you to show that you have listened to your editor's concern about profitability. And there are plenty of variables to play with – at what level of sales the step should be set, what the royalty rate should rise to, whether there should be more than one step, and so on.

6. Meta-text
   The question of which territory's laws a contract is made according to is an important one, but difficult to influence. Usually you would want the law to be that of your own territory – you are likely to know that law better and to be able to fight your corner more efficiently there – but if you are dealing with a foreign press

this will be difficult to achieve. At least ensure there is a clear statement of fact.

When you are negotiating, be unfailingly courteous: somehow, discourtesy tends to be self-defeating. Once, as a commissioning editor, I had lunch with an author in order to discuss a possible textbook about finance. Towards the end of the main course, he said to me, 'I always get my attorney to read my publishing contracts and, by the way, if you send me a contract, I won't be paying my attorney to read it: you will!' (At the point indicated by the colon, he pointed his finger across the table at me.) Strangely enough, he never received a contract from me – in fact, he wasn't even offered a pudding!

When you discuss the contract, be sure both to listen to the responses you receive and to show that you are listening. Even when they are not the responses you wanted, they may help you to see what is at stake for the other party and they may provide hints of ways forward.

Try to avoid backing yourself into a corner. Once when I was acting as an agent for an author, a commissioning editor who had offered a contract told us very early on in the process that the contract we had was a final offer. It was a question of 'take it or leave it': the contract 'couldn't be altered'. I did in fact succeed, very gradually, in gaining some revisions, but we decided to accept an offer from an alternative publisher. When I informed the unsuccessful editor, she was disappointed and even asked me whether there was anything she could have done differently. 'Yes', I said, 'not back yourself into a corner'.

It is useful, though often far from easy, to try to work out who you are actually negotiating with. Usually the editor will need to gain approval for contract changes, either from a director or from the company's contract department. Often, though, the editor will be authorised to make certain kinds of changes themselves. These are often the changes that are easiest to agree, though which they are can usually be ascertained only through a process of trial and error.

Above all, see the business of negotiating a contract as a learning process. Even if you gain no concessions, you are likely to gain at least a better understanding of the contract. And usually it is possible to improve the contract in *some* ways – even if they are minor. Then, the next time you negotiate a contract, you will start from a stronger position: you already know how to win some concessions and so can look to go farther. This ratchet effect means that, over a number of contracts, one can become increasingly proficient. And though many authors regard the prospect of negotiating as uninviting, it is possible to get a taste for it.

For ease of reference, Appendix C provides a summary of the above discussion of the structure of contracts and key questions for clarification and negotiation.

By now you may well be wondering whether authors need to do all this for themselves and, if so, whether there are any sources of advice. One option is to take advice from a lawyer. That should produce the most rigorous advice – though I would recommend consulting one who has experience of contracts in publishing and an acquaintance with the industry. The disadvantage of this option is, of course, the cost, which for the majority of academic books would be likely to exceed any income from royalties. You may, however, like to think of this as a loss leader, since you can learn from the advice that you receive on your first contract and then seek to apply it yourself on subsequent occasions.

An alternative option is to consult a professional association. For example, any writer in the UK who has been offered a publishing contract is entitled to apply for membership of The Society of Authors. The Society offers to vet contracts for members free of charge. As a member myself, I have made use of this service and, as an editor, I have worked with authors who have done the same: my impression is that the service is certainly helpful and justifies the (modest) cost of membership.

A further option is to use a literary agent. In a review of my first book, *Writing Successful Textbooks*, Professor Peter Atkins pointed out that I failed to discuss the role of literary agents. This was, I think, a fair criticism – so the next section is designed to ensure that it doesn't recur.

LITERARY AGENTS

There is a common assumption that the main role of literary agents is to earn their authors more money. It is certainly true that agents aim to do just that. And I dare say that, on most occasions, agents do indeed manage to improve the financial terms involved in a deal. On some academic books, such as major textbooks and trade books, the financial gain may be sizeable. However, we should bear in mind that agents charge their authors commission. In the case of many academic books, where there are only modest amounts to play for, the benefit of the enhanced terms that the author has negotiated with the publisher might be taken up by the cost of the agent's commission.

It does not follow, however, that in such circumstances it's not worth engaging an agent. For one thing, you are buying the agent's time, leaving your own free to progress your academic work. For another, a number of benefits can accrue from having an agent, besides financial gain. Let's consider each of these in turn.

First, agents can improve their authors' chances of getting published. An agent can discuss with an author which ideas might be worth developing into a fully fledged proposal and which should be left to wither on the vine. When it comes to developing the proposal, the agent can provide advice on what to include – and what not to. As someone who has occasionally agented authors myself, I am confident that the advice I've given authors at proposal stage has sometimes led to the project being contracted rather than rejected. To academic authors, this may be a greater benefit than any financial gain.

Moreover, agents may help their authors not only to find publishers, but to find the most appropriate publishers for their books. They can also help to improve the non-financial conditions in the publishing contract, as well as the terms. As we have seen above, these may be significant. Agents also help to ensure that publishers pay royalties promptly, and check royalty statements to make sure that they are accurate.

Another benefit of having an agent is that it frees the author to develop a relationship with their editors based on their writing. Conversations between editors and agented authors need not be punctuated with discussion about whether a certain clause in the contract can be changed or whether the advance will be paid on time. Instead, they can focus on editorial and literary matters, such as style, language, structure, and ideas.

Finally, quite apart from dealings with the publishing industry, having an agent can be of direct benefit to authors. Authors like to feel that they have someone alongside them to exchange ideas, provide support and encouragement, share enthusiasm, and, where necessary, chivvy to ensure that deadlines are met. The agent can also help to do what I hope this book does too – namely, explain and interpret the way the book industry works.

If you are considering using an agent, be aware that obtaining one may be far from easy. Agents have limited capacity: each agent can handle only so many authors at any one time (say, three dozen). The number of authors who wish to have an agent seems somehow always to exceed agencies' capacities. Thus the decision to take an author onto the books entails an opportunity cost for the agent, because s/he will always have to turn down other authors as a result.

An academic author who is writing a book that has genuine potential to cross over into the consumer market may be able to attract an agent. An author who is writing a textbook with major adoption potential may also be successful. In both cases, the odds of finding an agent will be improved if the author has already established a successful publishing record. If, however, an author is writing academic books with limited market potential – typically monographs or supplementary texts – it will be difficult to attract an agent.

If you decide to seek an agent, it is important to ensure that you approach agencies that are professional and have expertise in your area. Agency is not regulated in the way that professions such as law and medicine are. One can't just decide to market oneself as, say, a lawyer or a surgeon – one needs first to obtain recognised qualifications – but there is nothing to stop anyone from setting up as an agent. One does occasionally hear horror stories as a result. Jim Fisher tells one such story in a book entitled *Ten Percent of Nothing: The Case of the Literary Agent from Hell.*

Fortunately, it is not difficult to steer clear of the sharks. There are professional bodies designed to promote professionalism amongst agents. For example, in the UK, the Association of Authors' Agents (AAA) applies qualifying criteria to agents wishing to become members. For instance, prospective members must have at least two years' experience of agency. The AAA also requires members to abide by a code of practice. The code requires members, for example, to respect client confidentiality and to ensure that they have adequate indemnity insurance. Similarly, the professional association in America, the Association of Authors' Representatives (AAR), has established a 'Canon of Ethics'.

It does not follow that any agent who is not a member of the AAA or AAR (or their equivalents in other territories) is unprofessional. It may be that the agent's business is simply too new to qualify. Neither does it follow that being represented by a professionally recognised agent will turn out to be a wonderful experience. One risk for academic authors is that, if the sales projections for their books are modest, an agent may in practice devote more time to other, more marketable, authors. As a commissioning editor, I have occasionally (though thankfully not often) dealt with academic authors who, it seemed clear to me, were not receiving a good service from their agents, who seemed somehow always to be attending to some business other than the author's. In each case, the author was a big name within academia, yet (despite some wider name recognition) not well known to the general public.

If you are considering agency representation and receive interest from a prospective agent, it is important to meet in person if at all possible. Assess not only whether the agent seems well informed and proficient in general, but also whether s/he has experience and expertise in the type of market you are involved with. An agent may, for example, be an expert in dealing with novels or celebrity memoirs, but lack experience in, say, textbook publishing. Note that more than just business considerations are involved: representation involves a personal relationship between author and agent. Use a prospective meeting to assess whether you feel comfortable with the agent, whether you are on the same wavelength, and whether you feel you can develop a relationship based on trust and mutual respect. In addition, ask around and establish whether other authors, especially authors comparable to you, are prepared to endorse the agent in question.

SUMMARY

1. If you are being commissioned to write a book, obtain a contract as soon as possible.
2. Read the entire contract.
3. Consider each detail of the contract in isolation and also consider how the contract hangs together as a whole.

4. Negotiate.
5. When negotiating, be courteous, seek to negotiate on more than one point at a time, and look for 'win-win' opportunities.
6. Consider taking advice.
7. Winning improved financial terms from a publisher is not an agent's sole function. It may not even be the most important one.
8. If you wish to be represented by an agent, take trouble to ensure that any agent you approach is professional, reputable, and experienced in the type of market you wish to publish in.

PART II

Writing the Text

CHAPTER 5

Processes (1)

In English, the word 'writing' may refer either to a product or a process. That is, we may use the word to mean either a text – as when we talk of some 'piece of writing' – or an activity ('I'm going to spend this morning writing'). One would think that writing as product and writing as process are sufficiently different for there to be no confusion between the two. In practice, though, it can be difficult to keep the two apart. One may start to think of 'writing' in the sense of process, only to find one's mind slips silently into thinking instead of writing as product.

For example, imagine you are writing the opening chapter of a monograph. You are engaged in the *process* of writing. Having written a few pages, you stop to review what you have produced (note how readily that word presents itself). You ask yourself, 'Have I got the tone right?' 'Is the style appropriate?' And, most of all, you ask yourself, 'Is this good enough?' That is, you begin thinking of your writing in terms of product – both the product of your labour to date and the finished product that you are aiming towards.

The good news is that this can be a productive thing to do. Your conception of how the finished product should read will provide criteria for making judgements about the text that you have produced so far. It will give you, for example, a sense of what sort of style is appropriate for this type of writing.

That is the good news. The bad news is that eliding writing as a process with writing as a product can also be a hindrance – in fact, one of the greatest hindrances that writers can inflict on themselves. Some writers are fortunate enough to be able to write very well at first sitting. Many more experience this good fortune from time to time. But for most writers, most of the time, this is not the case. Most authors' first drafts turn out to be way off beam. Typically they are beset with problems – clumsiness, omissions, inaccuracies, irrelevance, obscurity, wordiness, illogicality, errors of judgement, and so on. If one then measures drafts against some ideal standard of how the writing 'should' be, the result is likely to prove dispiriting. The blemishes of the draft are highlighted.

It is worse still if, as often happens, one finds oneself comparing one's writing with the ideal of the finished product, not once one has finished a draft but, rather, as one is actually writing. The gap between what is required and what is actually issuing from one's pen, as it were, is likely to prove too great.

Even worse, the despair may set in before one even begins to write. The gap between the idealised version and the initial text that one is likely to produce may seem so like a chasm that one concludes it is better to do something less futile instead – check one's e-mails, read an article, or make some coffee.

The problem arises because the elision of thought between the process of writing and the product isn't symmetrical. In the process of writing, writers often think of writing as a product. But when looking at products, we rarely think of the processes that lie behind them. We rarely get to read other people's first drafts. Even when a colleague asks for comments or advice on a draft, it's likely to be a reasonably well-advanced draft that is provided. With most published texts that we read – monographs, journal articles, and so on – we are unlikely to see anything of the drafts – or associated plans, false starts, scribbled notes, corrections, deleted text, and so on – that preceded them. What we see is the author's final version, enhanced by the professional efforts of copy-editors, peer reviewers, typesetters, proofreaders, and so on. Other people's writing seems then to come into the world fully formed and beautifully polished – only one's own writing, it seems, is amateurish.

There is one further nail to be added to the coffin of authorial ambition. The more one loses sight of writing as process and focuses on writing as product, the less attention one gives to the processes themselves – to what processes one uses, to how those processes work, and how they may be improved.

The solution to these difficulties is to THINK PROCESS. As an author myself, and as a mentor of academic authors, I know of no more liberating insight than this. It is liberating by virtue of the corollaries that follow from it. For if we think of writing as a process, we will see that:

1. no piece of writing is finished until we consider it so;
2. so long as writing is unfinished, it's capable of improvement;
3. no matter how poor one's original attempt at writing is, it is usually possible to see how it can be improved;
4. since the first draft is no more than a starting point, the quality of that draft is not of fundamental importance.

In short, when drafting a piece of writing, you may write as badly as you like. As an author, I remember the marvellous sense of release that follows from recognising the full force of this conclusion.

The rest of this chapter and the next are devoted to 'thinking process'. We will look at the processes that are involved in writing, how they work, and in what ways each process is significant. It should be said straightaway that authors are diverse, in terms of both the processes they use and what works best for them. It is impossible to describe, still less to prescribe, a set of processes common to all authors.

We can, however, outline processes that are fairly typical or, at least, widespread. We can also examine what they contribute and how they may be harnessed. For the sake of simplicity, we will group these processes into the following broad types:

1. incubation
2. planning and preparation
3. drafting
4. redrafting
5. checking
6. presentation.

The rest of this chapter will examine the first three of these processes. The remaining three will be examined in Chapter 5.

INCUBATION

Let us consider these phases one-by-one – though this is not, as we shall see, how writing itself usually progresses. The OED defines incubation as the 'phase through which germs of disease pass before the development of first symptoms'. For incubation in writing, we can create a parallel, less pathological, definition: we may say that incubation is the phase through which themes and ideas pass before expression in writing.

Incubation is the least understood of writing processes. It may vary hugely in duration. Some writers report, and biographers surmise, that ideas may germinate for decades. Incubation is perhaps the least conscious, least programmable, of writing processes. It often seems to occur at a subconscious level. Just as one's mind sometimes seems able to solve problems while one is asleep, so the incubation process often seems to continue whilst one is thinking of something else and is perhaps unaware of the process.

A process of indeterminate length that is difficult to control is an awkward one to incorporate into modern academic life. The structure of the latter is often premised on schedules and articulated objectives. If you were to say to your line manager, or to write as a part of a research bid, 'I am incubating a few half-formed ideas and am not quite sure what they're leading to, although I expect they'll result in some kind of outcome over the next few decades', you may not receive a sympathetic reception.

This doesn't mean, however, that the process of incubation has no bearing on academic authorship. It can, after all, prove an extraordinarily rich process. In particular, it can be a source of genuinely creative thought. In order to exploit the process, I recommend first of all that you learn to listen, as it were, to your inner voice. Just as people who develop a routine of recording their dreams when they first wake in the morning can improve their ability to recall dreams (or is it that they have more of them?), so noting the ideas forming in one's mind makes the incubation process more productive. Keeping a reflective journal in which to try to capture, or at least register, one's thought can, therefore, be rewarding.

One feature of academic life that is sympathetic to the process of incubation is the opportunity that it provides to change location. Academics travel to conferences and meetings, for example. Changes in location can be conducive to ideas bubbling up to the surface. Often this happens not during the formal part of whatever event one has travelled to – the conference papers, the presentations, or whatever – but in the margins: en route on the train, for example, or sitting in a café before the start of the working day. If and when such occasions do reveal an idea that your mind has been incubating for you, it is important not to let it escape. It is useful, therefore, to develop the habit of always carrying some means – a pen and note-pad, for example – of jotting things down as they occur to you.

Another way to develop and exploit the process of incubation is to take a successful piece of work you have completed and to analyse its genesis. Once, after I'd written some pieces about education, I sat down to work out how those pieces had come about. I found I could represent the contributions of various factors in the form of a flow diagram. The exercise revealed to me, that although my subject reading was an important influence on what I wrote, it was a less dominant factor than I had thought. I recognised that, for me, some other factors were significant: these included events, conversations with people, interdisciplinary contexts, and non-verbal or multime-dia stimuli. Once I had completed this exercise I began to accord more respect to such occurrences and, as a result, my creative capac-ity expanded.

PLANNING AND PREPARATION

Often the processes of planning and preparation are intertwined. Here, however, for the sake of clarity, we will consider them sequen-tially. Let's take planning first.

Authors tend to use the word 'planning' to refer to two types of activity. First, there is planning the text itself. This involves making preliminary decisions over the length the text will run to, the shape it will assume, how many parts it will consist of, and so on. This type of planning is synonymous with 'structuring'. Second, there is planning in the sense of project management. This involves deci-sions over matters such as when to write, where to write, who else to involve, and so on. Here we will discuss planning of the first sort, i.e. structuration; discussion of planning of the second type is reserved to Chapters 9 and 10.

Authors vary hugely in the amount of planning they do. Some will do no planning at all before beginning to write. This approach has certain advantages. It prevents procrastination: there is no danger of using planning as an excuse for postponing writing. It can also be useful as a heuristic method: by writing, one discovers what it is one actually wants to write about or to say. Yet the approach also has disadvantages. It often involves false starts or takes the writer off along tangents that in due course can be seen as irrelevant. Much deletion of text will follow. Whilst it may well be possible to write short pieces – blogs, for example – without planning, authors of longer pieces of text, such as books, are likely sooner or later to decide that some form of plan is required.

For most authors a lack of planning is, I suggest, a sign of immaturity. The adage that 'time spent planning is time well spent' is a good one. Where authors do write a long text without a plan, it is usually because there is some form of ur-text already in existence – for example, a presentation given previously that has enabled the author already to sketch out what the book will be about.

At the opposite extreme to not planning at all, some authors microplan their texts. For example, one author I mentor plans extensively and minutely, using Microsoft's Powerpoint programme. He begins by dividing topics and sub-topics into slides. As the process continues, he begins to add slides for smaller units of texts – sub-sub-topics, as it were. He also begins to fill in the detail of each slide, adding a bullet point for each point of the argument. In due course he adds data too – actual examples, figures, references, and so on. In the course of this process he is constantly making and revising decisions over such matters as what constitutes a topic, what order the slides should come in, and so on. Only when he has refined this process to the point where he feels it is complete and no further revisions are required does he begin to write the text in Word. By this stage, he will have constructed scores of slides. From then on, composition becomes a fairly mechanical task, consisting largely of converting the Powerpoint text into grammatical prose and adding linking phrases between sentences and paragraphs.

By way of contrast, let me describe how I planned the first book I wrote. The first stage of planning was to decide how to divide the book into chapters. The second stage was to decide how to divide each chapter into half a dozen or so sub-sections. In practice, this required some revision of my original decisions over chapters. I then used the long commute I had to think about each sub-section in turn. This activity was largely mental, though I did note down any phrases that had come into my head that I thought I might actually use in the text. I then used sessions of about two hours on Thursday evening and Saturday mornings to generate the prose.

The forementioned author and I are agreed that we would hate to write without planning. But clearly our methods are worlds apart. My method would drive him nuts, as his would me. In particular, I would find the actual writing of prose that has been so precisely planned beforehand to be a boring chore. He, on the other hand, feels at this stage like a jockey who has cleared the final hurdle and is free to gallop as hard as possible down the home straight. There is, of course, no single correct method. It is a question of finding what works for you – and what works is the only question that matters here.

One of the most widely used methods of structuration is listing. One writes first the main title, then the titles of the main sections, and then the titles for each sub-section. Based on this method, the plan for this chapter would look something like that shown in Box 5.1.

This method has certain advantages. It clarifies both the sequence and the logical hierarchy of topics. I suspect, however, that the

---

Box 5.1 List plan

The Processes of Writing

1. 'Writing'
   A) product
   B) process
2. Processes
   A) corollaries
   B) specification of processes
3. Incubation
4. Planning
   A) linear planning
   B) non-linear planning
5. Preparation
6. Drafting
7. Summary

method is popular not so much because of its advantages, but rather because it's simply the most widely taught. It is, after all, the way that students are often taught to write essays. The method does, however, have some disadvantages. It encourages linear thinking: typically one constructs the list in the same order that the reader will read the text, i.e. by starting at the top. Yet what constitutes the best order for the reader may not be the best order for the writer. Moreover, the method really makes only one form of relationship between components clear, namely scale (main points subsume sub-sections and so on). And questions of scale, with the accompanying apparatus of numbers and letters, can press on authors rather early in the process and come indeed to preoccupy them. However, if you find that the device of a list works well for you, there is no reason to abandon it. Each method has its own strengths and weaknesses.

As an alternative to the list, many authors prefer to use non-linear methods. The development of digital pens and tablets has made it easier for authors to incorporate such methods on screen. Probably the most widespread visual approach is the use of mind-mapping techniques, popularised by study skills experts such as Tony Buzan.

The advantages of mind-mapping are largely the flipside of the disadvantages of using a list: it frees the author from thinking linearly, from having to start at the top, and from having to make decisions about scale and logical hierarchy too early in the process. As a consequence, however, the writer can find that there remains a good deal of thinking to do when it comes to converting the mind map into prose.

An alternative visual method is the grid. On training courses I have found this method (which I often use myself) is popular, especially amongst authors who have been using the list technique but would like to find an alternative. The grid method is attractive because it may be made as simple or as complex as one wishes.

To use this method, first draw a grid consisting of three rows and three columns. Then write in a main topic in each box, as in Table 5.1. At this stage, this result may be nothing more than a list displayed as a grid rather than vertically. Yet one may make it more complex than this. For example, one may use the rows to mean something. And similarly with the columns. It helps here that

Table 5.1 *Grid*

TOPIC A	TOPIC B	TOPIC C
TOPIC D	TOPIC E	TOPIC F
TOPIC G	TOPIC H	TOPIC I

Table 5.2 *Complex grid*

	gold	*silver*	*bronze*
thesis	TOPIC A	TOPIC B	TOPIC C
antithesis	TOPIC D	TOPIC E	TOPIC F
synthesis	TOPIC G	TOPIC H	TOPIC I

many of the schemas we use to think about texts naturally divide into three. For example:

- beginning/middle/end
- thesis/antithesis/synthesis
- gold/silver/bronze (i.e. best point, second-best, third-best)
- positive/negative/interesting (a schema popularised by Edward de Bono)

Similarly, many disciplinary debates often focus on the relationships between three concepts or schools of thought. For example, the concepts of author/text/reader, Father/Son/Spirit, and id/ego/super-ego are often central in literary theory, Christian theology, and psychoanalysis respectively. Similarly the schemas of neoclassicalism/Keynesianism/Marxism and Durkheim/Marx/Weber have been central to debates in economics and sociology respectively.

Thus, numerous permutations are possible. Table 5.2, for example, shows a relatively complex grid in which the author has chosen to make each row and column mean something. It should be emphasised, however, that this degree of complexity is a matter of choice: it is not integral to the method. In the plan for this chapter, for example (shown in Table 5.3), I chose to make the use of neither rows nor columns meaningful. Next, one may add sub-topics or key phrases.

Table 5.3 *Grid for this chapter*

PRODUCT/PROCESS	PROCESSES	INCUBATION
PLANNING (i)	PLANNING (ii)	PLANNING (iii)
PREPARATION	DRAFTING	SUMMARY

Table 5.4 *Grid for this chapter (refined)*

'WRITING' Product/process	PROCESSES Corollaries Specification of processes	INCUBATION
PLANNING (i) Linear method	PLANNING (ii) Non-linear methods	PLANNING (iii) Questions Word budgets
PREPARATION	DRAFTING	SUMMARY

Take this chapter again as an example (see Table 5.4). Here we may add a further level of refinement by noting in each box the most salient details. That is, we may add a note about the key references, datasets, quotations, research findings, dates, or other kind of data to be included. For example, in the 'Incubation' box in Table 5.4, I could have added '*OED*' to indicate that I would cite the dictionary's definition of 'incubation'. Similarly, in the 'Planning (II)' box I could add 'Buzan' and 'De Bono' to indicate my intention to cite those thinkers.

In the above examples, we have applied the nine-point grid at the level of chapters. We should note, however, that it can be used for larger and smaller units (say, whole books or passages of prose, respectively). Indeed, a book can be planned as a nest of tables where each of the nine boxes for the top-level (i.e. whole-book) grid represents a table and may in turn itself become nine boxes (as in Table 5.3) on the meso-level (i.e. that of the chapter). A passage within a chapter may in turn be planned using a micro-level grid.

By this stage, one might well ask, 'Why *nine* boxes? What is so magical about the number nine?' The answer, of course, is that there is nothing magical about it. Naturally, one could use other numbers of boxes instead. Yet, before dispensing with the nine-box grid, we should note that it does have certain advantages. It is easy to remember. I find that using this method, I can plan pieces of writing, and remember the plans, without needing a screen or a piece of paper. The fact that nine is an odd number is perhaps too an advantage: because it's not divisible by two, it forces authors to move beyond rather boring structures, such as compare/contrast or similarities/differences, based on binary opposites. Somehow, the fact that the nine-box grid looks like a noughts-and-crosses board seems to bring out the ludic side of authors – and anything that makes writing more fun must be an advantage.

Regardless of the method of planning used – list, mind map, grid, or some other method – two further levels of refinement may be added. First, topics may be labelled with questions rather than words and phrases. For example, the list plan in Box 5.1 above may be replaced with one like Box 5.2.

Though the difference between using questions, and using phrases, as labels may seem merely semantic, my experience of mentoring authors suggests that the use of questions leads to more focused, more purposeful, writing. It also suits those authors (myself included) who like to know where a piece of writing is going but don't like to have every 'i' dotted and 't' crossed before starting to write.

The second type of refinement is so simple it might be thought too obvious to mention – except that in fact many authors have not encountered the idea. The idea is to add a word budget to a plan.

Box 5.2 Chapter plan based on questions

The Processes of Writing

1. 'Writing': how are writing-as-product and writing-as-process related?
2. Processes: what follows from seeing writing as a process? What processes are involved?
3. How may the following processes be characterised? How can authors implement them?
   a) Incubation?
   b) Planning and preparation?
   c) Drafting?
4. What are the key points arising from the chapter?

For example, let us suppose you are planning to write a 60,000-word book. You can then construct a word budget as follows. First, estimate the combined length of prelims (for example, the contents page and acknowledgements) and end matter (for example, notes and references). Let us say these will account for 6,000 words. That leaves 54,000 words for the main text. If you are planning to write ten chapters, that would allow an average of 5,400 words per chapter. The next step is to write this figure against each chapter. In practice, you are likely to decide that some chapters need more than the average amount and some need less. You can then, as it were, buy and sell words between chapters. For example, you can take 1,000 off one chapter and add them to another.

Adding a word budget to your plan yields a number of benefits. It provides a preliminary indication of whether your plan is in fact feasible. (If, for example, you find yourself thinking, 'I need more space to cover that topic properly' or 'I don't want to write that much on that topic', you know that you need to change the plan before you start writing – which is certainly preferable to discovering the problem once you have already written several thousand words.) A word budget also helps to provide milestones: when you are writing you can say to yourself comments such as 'Just another 1,700 words to go on this topic' or 'I'm 65 per cent of the way there.' Breaking a large task, such as writing a book, into smaller, more manageable units, usually proves motivating. A further benefit is that the word allocation for each topic serves as a reminder of how much you have space for.

Once you have estimated a word budget for the whole book and for the meso-level units (in most cases, chapters), you can then do the same at a micro-level (in most cases, sub-sections within chapters). If, for example, you have allocated 4,000 words to a chapter and it has six sub-sections, then you know you have 600–700 words per unit. Again, this helps you to check that your plan is feasible.

So far, in our budgeting, we have been working top-down. That is, we started with the largest unit (the book as a whole) and worked down to smaller units (first chapters, then sub-sections). However, we can complement this method by also thinking bottom-up. If you review examples of text you have written in the past, you can calculate: (a) the average length of your sentences (in terms of numbers of words): and (b) your average number of sentences per paragraph. You can then begin to see what a passage will look like, even before you have written it. Suppose, for example, you typically write about 17 words per sentence and 6 sentences per paragraph (and thus 100 words or so per paragraph). If you have budgeted, say, 650 words for a sub-section of your chapter, then you know you have space for half a dozen or so paragraphs.

If you have never tried planning text in this way, the bottom-up method may sound rather unrealistic. In fact, however, it usually takes very little time to get used to thinking in such terms. One can rapidly develop a feel for how many paragraphs are required for a certain passage of prose – and the more developed the feel, the less one actually needs to do the arithmetic. You find yourself saying something along the lines of: 'we need four or five paragraphs on this topic'.

This is not to suggest that one needs to think on this level – let us call it the nano-level – throughout the whole book. Nano-level thinking can on occasion prove fruitful – particularly if you find yourself feeling uncertain how to proceed with your writing or short of either confidence or motivation. If, for example, you find the prospect of writing a book, or even just a chapter, rather daunting, it can be very refreshing to say something along the lines of: 'I need to write four paragraphs on this topic and I need about five sentences in the first paragraph.' Though the end of the book may seem a long way off, the end of the paragraph needn't be.

So far in this section we have looked only at planning. What of preparation? It is important to be clear about what preparation is and is not. Preparation is the process of making writing as easy as possible. It involves clearing a space and marshalling one's resources. Preparation does not involve procrastination: it is the opposite. Printing the documents you know you will need to refer to whilst writing is an example of preparation: 'clearing e-mails' is not (you never clear them, anyway, since the sooner you send them off, the sooner the replies come in: the only solution is to turn your e-mail off). Neither is making yourself coffee, since that merely postpones the act of writing by another quarter of an hour and, despite what you may say to yourself, you don't actually 'need' a cup of coffee to start writing. You can make the coffee later, as a reward, once you've got a momentum going.

To distinguish preparation from procrastination one needs to be ruthlessly honest with oneself. I find the trick is to think very literally. When I say that preparation involves clearing a space, I mean quite literally making room on the desk (which can usually be done quickly and which clearly hastens the act of writing). I don't mean clearing a mental space, since that is likely to prove an inducement to indulging in meditation *instead of* writing. Similarly, by 'marshalling resources' I mean material resources – books, pens, memory sticks, documents, or whatever – rather than psychological ones. If in doubt, ask yourself whether an activity is in practice centripetal (pointing towards the activity of writing) or centrifugal.

When writing, it is desirable to anticipate likely breaks in concentration. It is undoubtedly productive to gather resources together in a convenient place at the start of a writing session. Ensure that the books you wish to refer to are within easy reach. Ensure that the computer documents you wish to cut and paste from are stored on your desktop. In your website favourites, create a folder specifically for each chapter: that way you can go straight to a webpage without being distracted by a search engine and lured into the farther reaches of the worldwide web.

It is best to stack books and documents in the order in which you wish to consult them, so that you don't lose concentration by having to shuffle texts. Similarly, it helps to mark pages, quotations, and so on with pieces of sticky paper.

DRAFTING

Drafting is the process that generates most text. It is tempting to think of it as the real work of writing. Indeed, inexperienced authors often reduce the writing process almost entirely to that of drafting text. The main thrust of this chapter, however, is to de-emphasise the role of drafting within the writing process.

Clearly, drafting is indispensable – without the text generated at this stage, an author would have no product. Yet drafting is but one stage in the overall authorial process – and the better one conducts the other stages, the less critical the work of drafting becomes and the easier it is to do.

To see how this is the case, try a thought experiment. Imagine that you are going to reduce the writing of a text to a single process. You will allocate no time at all to planning, to revising, to checking, or to anything else except sitting at the keyboard producing text. Now imagine the questions that will be going through your mind as you write.

Here are a few of them:

> Where is this going? Is that clear? Is this what I really think? Does that make sense? Have I got that right? How do you spell that? How long should this section be? Should I put that in the next chapter? What reference style do I use? Is this any good? How long do I want this book to be? Who am I writing for? Does the punctuation mark go inside the inverted commas or outside? Does that sound repetitious? Is that argument strong enough? Have I given enough examples?

… and so on and on. Cognitive overload or what? This is the kind of thing that undergraduates experience when they have an 'essay crisis', i.e. when they start to write an essay the night before it is due to be submitted. It may be possible to work like this when all that is required is a 1,000-word essay – although, even then, it is an unpleasant and often ineffective way to work – but clearly it isn't the way to go about professional authorship. This way of working gives the writer far too many things to think about at once. It also raises too many different *kinds* of things to think about. The above question about punctuation, for example, clearly requires a completely different kind of thinking from, say, the question of whom one is writing for. Trying to do all this at once is a recipe for nervous breakdown.

Now, of course, by the time authors turn to writing books they will have developed a more considered, gradualist, approach. They will certainly devote time to planning, to revising, and to checking. They will, therefore, take some of the pressure away from the drafting stage of the process. The question is, do they go far enough?

As always with writing, this comes down to a question of what works. If in your own case, you find you have already developed a set of processes that works effectively for you, then that's the end of the problem. If, however, when it comes to drafting text, you lack confidence or find the process difficult or unenjoyable, the solution may be to think more radically about how you go about the process.

The purpose of drafting is to generate text – lots of it. Drafting is the stage of the process where the blank sheet of paper becomes covered with blue ink or the white screen becomes filled with black font. Drafting, therefore, is primarily about quantity. In this, it is unlike other stages in the authorial process. For example, the later stage of checking what you have written is purely concerned with quality: checking is purely a means of quality management. Drafting, however, is about productivity, measured by the number of words generated. If, when you are drafting text, you happen to write well, that is very good news indeed. It means you will have less work to do on the text later in the process. But writing well at this stage is strictly a bonus: it isn't essential. The main purpose of drafting is to produce material that, in subsequent stages of the authorial process, you can then improve. If, in order to get that material out onto the page, you have to lower the bar and write text way below publishable standard, then you should not hesitate to do so. Whilst there is no point writing badly for the sake of it, you should certainly give yourself permission to do so if that is what gets you onto the next page. Where drafting is concerned, not to write well does not count as failure: not to write enough, does.

If you set out merely to write a lot, there is one quirk of human psychology that will help you. This is that the writing process itself generates ideas. Academia sometimes blinds itself to this fact through a fixation with the phrase 'writing up'. Researchers learn in graduate school to talk of 'writing up', as if they should do all their thinking first and then, after two or three years, merely transcribe it. There are certain situations in which it is perfectly legitimate to talk of writing in terms of transcription, but they relate almost wholly to short-term, relatively discrete tasks. Larger-scale, more open-ended, writing projects – such as writing either a dissertation or a book – rarely feel like acts of mere transcription. Typically what happens during the writing process is that one's thinking changes. Ideas refine, alter, or extend themselves and, crucially, lead to further ideas. Writing is as much a medium for thinking as it is a way of recording pre-ordered thought. The good news for any author engaged in drafting text is that writing thus has a habit of perpetuating itself, generating ever more text as it goes.

SUMMARY

1. Think of writing not only as a product, but also as a process.
2. Foster the incubation of ideas by (a) keeping a notebook to hand, (b) writing a reflective journal, and (c) modelling the processes by which your mind creates its best work.

3. Time spent planning is usually time well spent.
4. Writing may be planned either linearly or non-linearly.
5. Plans that incorporate questions often produce focused writing.
6. Prepare to write by ensuring that you have the necessary resources to hand and in good order.
7. When drafting, focus on productivity. Think quantity.

CHAPTER 6

Processes (II)

In the previous chapter we examined three authorial processes: (1) incubation; (2) planning and preparation; and (3) drafting. Here we will examine three further processes, namely (4) redrafting, (5) checking, and (6) presentation. Before we consider each of these phases in turn, however, it will help to stand back and consider the nature of writing in general. To do this, we will use two metaphors that between them seem to me to capture much of the phenomenology of writing. These metaphors are built around images of (a) a maze and (b) a sheepdog.

THE MAZE

First, consider a conventional maze – one consisting of numerous paths separated by hedges. Most of the paths are dead-ends. There is only one way to the centre. Usually there is some distinctive feature to mark the centre – a statue, say. Each fork in the path presents the visitor with a decision, yet unless one has completed the maze before there is really no way of knowing which is the right path to take. It is a question of trial and error. And if you succeed in getting to the centre, finding your way out again can be difficult. You might begin to fear that you will be lost forever.

Now consider a less conventional maze – one with, as it were, more than one centre. Let's say there are three of them – each marked as a destination by a distinctive symbol. In addition, there are again a number of dead-ends.

Finally, consider a still less conventional maze. I have in mind here one particular maze, which is to be found on some common land in Saffron Walden, a market town in the east of England. The maze, known as the turf maze, consists not of hedges but of lines cut in the ground. One can, therefore, see across the maze, which is about 30 metres in diameter. In principle, therefore, you can, without needing to enter the maze itself, see where each line in the maze will take you – provided that you concentrate hard enough. On investigation, one discovers that there is in reality only one line, though as it twists to and fro you could easily be misled into thinking there were more than one. In this maze, then, there are no dead-ends: there is a single line that leads, eventually, to the centre.

Now let's create an imaginary maze consisting of an amalgam of the second and third of the mazes above. As in the second maze, there is more than one centre and also a number of dead-ends. But as in the third maze, there are no hedges: the maze consists of lines cut in the ground and, with care, one can trace each line with the eye.

Writing is rather like negotiating this last maze. When we are writing, as when negotiating a maze, we are constantly presented with choices. For example, two words are synonymous – which of the two should we use? The next sentence could be written in either the active or the passive: which should it be? Should we bring one sentence to a conclusion and start another – or should we keep the first sentence going and add another clause to it? And so on. On each occasion, there is a decision to be made. Some decisions will prove to be bad ones, leading the text off in unprofitable directions. They equate with the dead-ends in the maze. Other decisions will lead the text towards a successful conclusion, though, since there is usually no pre-ordained shape that the text must follow, there are a number of alternative possibilities. That is, when an author sits down to write a book, there are a number of different forms that book might take (or, if you like, a number of different books the author might write), each of which may be successful in its own way. These alternatives equate to the various different 'centres' of the maze. With some forethought, you can discern in which direction each decision will take you: there are, as it were, no hedges. And if you find you are unhappy with the direction you have taken, you can, because of the lack of metaphorical hedges, always retrace your steps – or simply step out of the maze altogether and start again.

It will help, at this point, to consider an example. Let's take the paragraph above about the maze in Saffron Walden. Here again is the text that I ended up writing, though this time with the sentences numbered for ease of reference:

(1) Finally, consider a still less conventional maze. (2) I have in mind here one particular maze, which is to be found on some common land in Saffron Walden, a market town in the east of England. (3) The maze, known as the turf maze, consists not of hedges but of lines cut in the ground. (4) One can, therefore, see across the maze, which is about 30 metres in diameter. (5) In principle, therefore, you can, without needing to enter the maze itself, see where each line in the maze will take you – provided that you concentrate hard enough. (6) On investigation, one discovers that there is in reality only one line, though as it twists to and fro you could easily be misled into thinking there were more than one. (7) In this maze, then, there are no dead-ends: there is a single line that leads, eventually, to the centre.

This text is, for better or worse, the result of a multitude of decisions. Here are some that I remember making. In (1) I hesitated to write 'still less conventional'. I wondered whether the maze was really less conventional than the multi-centred maze I had mentioned previously. Momentarily I considered writing instead something along the lines of 'a maze that is unconventional in a different way'. But I rejected this alternative, in part because it sounded clunky and pedantic (and so may be considered a dead-end) and in part because I decided that, since I am writing a book about writing rather than mazes, it didn't matter a great deal which I chose: nothing hung on the decision. That is, the direction I chose might not be the only successful choice, but I judged it successful enough in its own way.

In (2) I was unsure whether to name the town in which the turf maze was to be found. I was going to omit the name because it seemed somewhat irrelevant. But in fact I decided to include it – in part because it provided a little local colour, in part because it made it easier to refer back to. A phrase such as 'maze in Saffron Walden' is more distinctive than, say, just 'turf maze'.

Let's consider one more example from the above paragraph. In (6) I originally wrote that the line in the maze 'twists to and fro over a course of 1,500 metres', but I then decided to omit the phrase 'over a course of 1,500 metres' because it was irrelevant. That such a long line is condensed into a circle about 30 metres in diameter is no doubt remarkable, but the fact is not pertinent to the metaphor I was developing. It was, therefore, a dead-end, though one that was easy enough to back out of.

I offer the metaphor of the maze for a number of reasons. It heightens one's awareness of the continual decision-making involved in writing; it encourages one to look ahead whilst writing and at each step to consider where the path is leading; and it reminds one that none of the decisions taken is actually irrevocable – a comforting thought that helps one not to come to a halt in the writing process for fear of making the wrong decision.

THE SHEEPDOG

The second metaphor occurred to me when I was taking a walk in the mountains of mid-Wales one November morning (local colour again, and quite irrelevant I admit!). A farmer was moving a flock of sheep from one field to another. I watched the scene from some distance and am not certain I properly understood what I was seeing – though since I am writing about writing and not about sheep-farming, the accuracy of my observation doesn't greatly matter.

When I started to watch, there were two dogs involved in the process. One was a collie. I'm not sure what breed the second dog was, but I do know it was having a whale of a time helping – or attempting to help – with the sheep. It was running up and down, to and fro, wagging its tail vigorously as it did so. Eventually, its owner – a woman who was perhaps the farmer's wife – decided to move on, taking the dog with her. The collie, who was clearly the farmer's sheepdog, then quietly got on with the business of moving the sheep into the next field. I say 'quietly' because there was no fuss – and certainly no further tail-wagging.

This seemed to me to provide the perfect metaphor for the work of writing – in the case of the collie, what writing should be like, and in the case of the second dog, what it all too often is actually like.

Perhaps I should be more explicit. The strategy, if such it could be called, of what we might call the amateur sheepdog seemed to be to wait and see where the sheep went and then, if it looked as if they were heading in the wrong direction, to spend a good deal of energy rushing after them, ensuring they would go back to the straight and narrow. The strategy of the professional, i.e. the collie, seemed rather to be to anticipate where the sheep might head off to, to position itself to prevent them from beginning to do so, and so ensure that they in fact ended up in the right place. The amateur's strategy was unsustainable – with all the energy expended, it would have worn itself out in no time. The collie, in contrast, looked as though he could keep it up all day, no sweat.

For 'sheep', read 'readers' (though with no offence intended). When the writing is amateur, readers are forever heading off in the wrong directions. They don't see where they are supposed to be going; they get the wrong end of the stick; they get ideas from the text, but not the ones the writer intended them to have. And, as you may well appreciate if you have ever circulated a carelessly phrased memo or e-mail, once readers have misunderstood you, it can be a devil of a job to retrieve the situation. Removing misunderstanding from the minds of readers, once it has arisen, requires a good deal of time and effort.

The work of the writer, therefore, is like that of the collie. The writer needs to understand the readers of a text as well as possible; to try to guess what is in their minds; to look ahead; and, above all, to anticipate difficulties and thus to prevent them arising.

Again, an example will help. Here again is the paragraph about the maze in Saffron Walden, though this time with some variations:

(1) Finally, consider a still less conventional maze. (2) I am thinking of one particular maze, which is to be found cut into some common land in Saffron Walden, a market town in the east of England. (3) The maze, known as the turf maze, consists not of hedges but of lines cut in the ground. (4) One can, therefore, see across the maze, which is about 30 metres in diameter. (5) In principle, therefore, you can, without needing to enter the maze itself, see where each line in the maze will take you – provided that you concentrate hard enough. (6) In fact one discovers that there is only one line, though as it curls to and fro you could easily be misled into thinking there were more than one. (7) In this maze, then, there are no dead-ends: there is a single line that leads, eventually, to the centre.

This version comes from an earlier draft. Here (2) begins not with the phrase 'I have in mind' but 'I am thinking of'. Though the original phrase makes sense, it is slightly misleading. We tend to use the phrase 'I am thinking of' when the reader already knows about the thing that the writer proceeds to refer to. If readers of this text had already heard of the maze in Saffron Walden, there would be no problem. 'Ah, yes', they would think as I continued the sentence, 'that maze, I know the one you mean'. But in fact only a minority of the readers of this book wll know of the maze. Some of those who had not heard of it would continue reading, perhaps simply unaware that the phrase 'I am thinking of' carried such a nuance. But some might just think, however fleetingly, 'Eh? Am I supposed to have known of that maze already? Does it matter if I haven't?' Though the phrase 'I am thinking of' wouldn't be wrong exactly – it certainly doesn't infringe any rule of grammar – it risks momentarily arousing an unfulfilled expectation.

I wrote in (2) that the maze was 'cut into some common land'. I later revised this to 'is to be found on some common land'. The problem with the original draft, of course, is that 'cut' is not a verb one usually associates with mazes. (One is more likely to talk of growing them.) The risk is that readers will be disconcerted. 'Cut?' they might well think, 'what does he mean by that?' Such confusion will be only momentary: they have only to read (3) to see what is meant. For a space of a dozen words or so, however, readers will have experienced a sense of uncertainty.

I have also rewritten (6). For example, I originally wrote 'curls' but then in the second draft replaced it with 'twists'. The problem with 'curls' is that it suggests a leisurely movement on the part of the line. 'Twists' suggests a sharper movement. It is preferable not merely because it more accurately describes the actual maze but also, more pertinently, because it emphasises that concentration is needed to trace the path of the line. That emphasis is important to the metaphor, because I wanted eventually to suggest that, while writers can look ahead and see where their decisions will lead them, this requires mental effort: good writing cannot usually be produced lazily.

It will be noticed that the above examples are each in themselves quite minor. None of the original variants could be termed wrong, exactly. The problems are merely ones of nuance. Over the course of a chapter, however, one might well present readers with scores of such local difficulties. And over the course of a book, there may well be hundreds or even thousands. Even if each instance is minor, the cumulative effect may be considerable. Before one knows it, the sheep have strayed all over the mountainside. The more one trains oneself to write the way the collie has been trained to herd sheep, the sooner the second dog is free to wander off home.

A common view of writing is that redrafting is a minor activity. Drafting, according to this view, is where the heavy-lifting is done. Redrafting consists merely of tidying the text up, giving it a bit of a polish or, to mix metaphors, putting icing on the cake.

If you write draft text well enough in the first place to be able to assign such a minor role to the redrafting stage of writing, then you are fortunate and unusual. For many writers, however, it is not like that. Authors often reach a fulcrum point in their writing development where the main emphasis switches from drafting to redrafting. (In my own development, it was only when I reached this point that I felt I could make any kind of claim to be a mature writer.) For such authors, it is at the redrafting stage that authorial skill really kicks in – and it is the work done at this stage that enables them to look other skilled people – lawyers or accountants or medics, for example – in the eye and say, 'I'm a professional too.'

Though the process of redrafting is often complex and requires skill, it is in essence simple to describe. Most redrafting involves one or more of the following operations:

Cutting text down or cutting it out
Adding
Changing text around

Before this, however, it is sometimes necessary simply to *review* passages of the text so that a decision can be made over which of the above three types of operation is called for.

A straightforward way to begin to redraft text is to read through the draft, annotating it in the margin as you do so. It is helpful to develop a set of symbols to enable you to annotate quickly, to avoid losing the flow of your reading. The symbols in Table 6.1 are simple yet powerful.

Having annotated draft copy in this way, you may prefer to redraft the text by working through it sequentially from top to bottom, reacting to each annotation in turn. Alternatively, you may adopt a

Table 6.1 *Symbols*

Symbol	Operations
↓	Reduce; edit down; make more concise; omit
↑	Expand; extend; say more; add to this
↔	Change around; alter; transform
⚲	Diagnose; look at more closely to decide what treatment is required

more systematic approach, dealing with all the instances of one symbol (e.g. all the '↓'s) before moving onto the next symbol.

Reducing

There is much to be said for dealing first with the '↓' passages. These tend to be the hardest from a psychological point of view. Most writers, having spent time and effort generating text, are somewhat reluctant to delete it. Draft text, however, can almost always – in fact, let me suggest, *always* – benefit in some way from cutting down. Think of this process as pruning: cutting out the dead wood invigorates your text and creates space for it to grow anew.

Before cutting any text, be sure to save a copy of the original. This has the practical advantage of enabling you to restore text if you change your mind about any of the cuts. More important is the psychological advantage: the security provided by retaining a copy of the original emboldens writers to make cuts in the first place.

Reductions in the text may entail changes on either a 'macro' or 'micro' scale. Macro cuts are extensive. They involve the excision of whole passages. First drafts often contain many tangents. Some passages seem relevant whilst you are writing them but, once the draft is complete, no longer so. Other passages may amount to no more than the written equivalent of throat-clearing: they helped the writer to get going but have no lasting value.

When removing passages, it can be useful to cut and paste the excised text into newly created documents. Such passages are not necessarily valueless: the problem with them may be that they just don't belong in the text you're currently working on. In due course, however, they may form the basis of new texts. Again, there is a psychological advantage to be gained as well as a practical one: the knowledge that any text you cut might in future be used in some other way can make the writer more willing to admit that they are out of place at present.

Micro cuts are those involving small segments of text – a word here, a phrase or clause there. Academic writing often contains much padding. Wordy phrases such as 'It should be noted that' or 'in relation to' abound. In an excellent essay entitled 'Loose, baggy sentences', Claire Kehrwald Cook argues that 'You can almost detect a wordy sentence by looking at it – at least if you can recognize weak verbs, ponderous nouns, and strings of prepositional phrases.' She shows how weak verbs, such as 'to be' and 'to have', often lead to rambling constructions. For example, forms of the verb 'to be' frequently feature in what Cook terms 'leisurely sentence openers' – 'It is important to note that …', 'There is …', and so on. My own first drafts abound with sentences beginning 'It is important …': when I re-read them, they make me yawn.

Cook also shows how academic writing 'sags under bulky nouns – especially long Latinate ones with endings like *tion* and *ment* and *ence*'. These often result from a process known as (to venture a *tion* word myself) nominalisation, whereby verbs are converted into nouns. For example, rather than write 'data was collected by', we might open a sentence by writing 'The collection of data …' – in which case the sentence will be well on the way to long-windedness. Nominalisation is one of the hallmarks of academic writing and it is by no means always a negative: indeed, it may facilitate abstract thought. Often, however, it leads to wordiness.

Cook shows too how frequently the use of prepositional phrases results in wordiness. Constructions such as 'in connection with', 'in order to' and 'in view of the fact' are staples of academic writing, yet commonly result in bagginess. The same may be said of verbal phrases such as 'is indicative of' (as opposed to 'indicates').

This is not a book about English usage, so I will resist the temptation to list more examples. Many such guides are available, however: the notes to this chapter recommend some of the best. The salient point here is that the kinds of wordiness outlined above pervade academic writing. It follows that the cumulative gains to be made from reducing text at the micro-level are often large. Over the course of an entire book one can often save several thousand words simply by getting rid of the padding.

When you are editing draft copy, it may be that, like Cook, you think in grammatical categories (e.g. prepositional phrases). Not everyone does, however. I find it is sufficient simply to divide text into parts that are 'alive' and parts that are 'inert'. By 'inert' I mean any bits of language (regardless of grammatical category) that are just dull or lifeless. It may be, for example, an adverb such as 'significantly' (often used by writers to claim the reader's attention, though frequently with the opposite result), or a conjunction such as 'however' (often used to mean nothing more than 'oh, and another thing…'), or a verb such as 'address' (increasingly becoming a sleep-inducing default verb): what they have in common is they just sit there on the page, doing nothing but getting in the way. Simply posing the question 'Which bits of my text are inert?' may be enough to help you spot words or phrases that can go. If, in the process, you delete between five and ten words in every hundred, that wouldn't be at all unusual.

Adding

One reason why text often needs to be expanded during the redrafting process is to make one's reasoning more explicit. Often when, as an editor, I read an author's draft text I find myself writing 'elliptical' in the margin. I do this where the argument that the author is pursuing may be correct and defensible, but some of the links are hidden from the reader. Such text is like a chain that is partially buried in the sand – for the part that lies above the ground, you can follow the line link-by-link but you lose the line when it goes underground. When it resurfaces you are unsure whether it's same chain.

The cause of elliptical writing is usually an under-estimation of the demands of the writer's subject matter vis-à-vis one's readers' knowledge. If you have been studying a subject for a number of years, it's very easy to forget just how much you have had to learn. As a result, you may assume things to be perfectly obvious that in fact need to be spelt out. Bear in mind that you do not usually know exactly who your readers will be. Some may be your peers – people whom you know through research conferences, who read the same journals, and so on: they may well be on the same wavelength as you. Other readers, however, will be at different stages in their careers, working in different contexts and perhaps different disciplines. They will require more guidance.

When redrafting your text, it is useful, therefore, to keep asking yourself, 'Where do I need to be more explicit?' If in doubt, try expanding the text. The responses of your readers to more explicit argumentation will be asymmetrical: readers who require explicitly argued text stand to benefit greatly, whereas those who do not are unlikely to be greatly inconvenienced. Readers who find text over-explicit are merely likely to be slowed down a little – and in any case they can always skip.

Another reason for expanding text is to enable you to repeat yourself. It is often said, of course, that repetition in writing is a bad thing. So it is, if the repetition serves no useful purpose. In a short piece of writing, such as an essay, there may be no need for repetition. However, over the course of an entire book, consisting of tens of thousands of words, repetition may be very useful. Readers may be grateful for the reminder or confirmation that repetition provides. Repetition, therefore, needs not so much to be avoided as to be controlled. When you think it may be useful to repeat yourself, ask yourself what the function of the repetition is. Also find ways of acknowledging and signposting the repetition by using such phrases as 'It may be helpful here to recap' or 'We should recall'.

Text also often needs to be extended in order to supplement theoretical explanation with concrete examples. Readers learn in different ways: some learn mainly through abstract reasoning, theoretical argument, the articulation of general principles, and so on; others learn more effectively from more concrete means, such as case studies, illustrations, and worked examples. A problem arises from the fact that authors tend to assume that readers learn in the same mode that they themselves learn – so, for example, authors who like to learn through theory will often write in a purely theoretical mode. If this applies for you, you should, when redrafting your text, look for opportunities to drop in more concrete material. Whilst you may find such material redundant ('If you've understood the theory, what's the point of examples?' you may be saying to yourself), some of your readers will be gasping for it.

Note that if you are writing in a theoretical subject, it does not follow that all of your writing need be in theoretical idiom. There is a distinction to be made between the *subject matter* of your writing and the *mode of presentation*. Even when you are writing about theory, there is usually an opportunity to show what that theory looks like in practice – that is, to illustrate it concretely, for example by quoting sample text from theoretical readings.

Another reason why text may need to be extended arises from authors' modesty. Good, original ideas are hard to come by, yet often when authors do produce some creative thinking, they fail to make the most of it. An author comes up with a good idea, floats it in their text, and then promptly allows it to disappear from view. As an editor, I am amazed at how often I find authors burying their best ideas. Perhaps the author thinks, 'Well, it's only my idea, so it probably isn't *really* important.' Journalists tend to be much better at exploiting promising openings: once they've found the really interesting point of a story, they will tend to run with it. If you think you might have a gem, don't be shy: flaunt it!

Changing text around

We have looked at the processes involved in (a) reducing text and (b) adding to it. Now let us consider a third set of processes, namely those involved in changing text around.

To help to identify the ways in which text needs to be changed around when it is redrafted, I've devised a series of diagnostic questions. To apply them effectively, it is important first to place oneself in the shoes of one's reader. Ask first, 'How would one of my target readers see this text?' and, only then, 'What do I need to change?'

The diagnostic questions are arranged in sets, each of which has a specific focus. The first focus is the conceptual content. When examining your draft text, ask yourself:

- What concepts are involved here? How difficult are they in themselves?
- How much elucidation does each concept require? Have any concepts not been presented clearly?

- What is the argument? How complicated is it? How evident is the logic?

These questions may lead you to devote more space or care to the manner in which you introduce concepts. For example, you may consider whether to include either a formal definition when a concept is first used or a glossary of key terms at the back of the book. The questions may also lead you to insert connectives (e.g. 'therefore', 'thus', 'nevertheless') to clarify the logical structure.

The second focus is the lexis of the text. The questions use the word 'lexeme' as shorthand for 'word or phrase'. Ask yourself:

- Which lexemes might be unfamiliar?
- Which lexemes might cause confusion?
- Where have different lexemes been used as synonyms? How clear is that they are synonymous? Would it be better to use just one of the lexemes?
- Where has a lexeme been used to mean different things on different occasions? How clear are the distinctions? Would it be better to employ a range of lexemes?

These questions might lead you to change the selection of lexemes you deploy. (For example, in the above questions I could have replaced 'lexeme' with 'word or phrase'.) They might also lead you to use terminology more consistently, perhaps seeking a one-to-one correspondence between lexemes and concepts (each lexeme referring to only one concept; each concept referred to by only one lexeme).

The third focus concerns the sentence structure. Ask yourself:

- How lengthy are the sentences?
- How complex (grammatically) are the sentences?
- Which are the most difficult sentences to read? (A good way to test this is to read aloud.)
- Which sentences are most difficult to understand or most open to misinterpretation?
- Where is the grammar unclear?

These questions frequently lead to simpler, shorter sentences. For example, you may find that you have written a compound sentence in which two main clauses are linked together by 'and'. Often replacing the 'and' with a full stop will produce more readable text. When you encounter a particularly lengthy sentence in your text, read through it and count how many opportunities there are to bring the sentence to an end by inserting a full stop. The more such opportunities that exist, the more likely your readers would be grateful to you for inserting the full stop.

The fourth focus concerns discourse structure. This involves looking at larger units of text (e.g. paragraphs or passages), rather than just lexemes or sentences. It is surprisingly easy to overlook larger-scale questions when you are working through your own text. Ask yourself:

- How clear is it what genre the text belongs to?
- How clear are the links between paragraphs? Where do the links need to be more explicit?
- How clear are the links between passages? Where do the links need to be more explicit?
- How clear is the purpose of each passage?
- Where would it help to include an explanation of how the text is organised?
- Where would more cross-referencing be beneficial?

These questions may lead you to insert more meta-text – that is, text about text. (For example: 'Now that we have considered the argument in favour of this hypothesis, we need to consider three possible objections.') They may also lead you to provide more headings or to introduce a numbering system. You may also find you want to introduce text that echoes or even repeats an earlier piece of text in order to make the writing more cohesive.

The final focus concerns context. This involves a consideration of the text in relation to factors beyond the text. Ask yourself:

- How effectively has the text been placed in context (for example, in relation to a wider intellectual debate)?
- How much allowance has been made for readers working in different contexts (for example, in different disciplines or cultures)? Do readers require more support from the text?
- Have enough intertextual links been provided (that is, links to other texts in the literature, for example through quotation, reference, allusion, or debate)? Do any of the intertextual links need to be made more explicit?

These questions may lead you to adopt a more patient approach, spending more time filling in the bigger picture and helping the reader to get their bearings.

Let us say you have drafted and redrafted your text. You've looked at it carefully, added material here, taken out material there, moved text around and revised it – and now you're happy with it. It's tempting at this stage to say to oneself, 'That's it: it's done now.' But it is important to resist that temptation, for two further processes lie ahead: namely, checking the text and presenting it.

When, at the beginning of his book *Writing And The Writer*, Frank Smith examines the meaning of the verb 'to write', he points out that:

Two people might in fact claim to be writing the same words at the same time, although each is doing different things. An author dictating to a secretary or into a tape recorder could claim to be writing a book without actually putting a mark on paper. The secretary or person doing the transcribing could also claim to be writing the same words, by performing a conventional act with pen, pencil, or typewriter.

From this we can deduce that there are two main roles involved in writing, namely (a) composer and (b) secretary. The composer is concerned with such matters as getting ideas and developing them, structuring the discourse, and so on. The secretary is concerned with such matters as recording text on paper or in digital form, checking the spelling and punctuation, getting the capital letters in the right place, and so on. In many ways, the shift from redrafting text to checking it forms a fulcrum. Up to this point, the skills of composing have been dominant: now, however, secretarial skills become more important.

Before starting to check your text, it is helpful to allow some time to elapse after redrafting it. This will help you to see the text with fresh eyes when you return to it. It's also a good idea to change the physical form of the text, for example by creating hard copy: when the text actually looks different, it's easier to notice points you haven't seen previously. Double-spacing the text helps you to see exactly what you have written and gives you room to annotate the text and insert corrections.

Attitude is important. There is a temptation at this stage to say to oneself, 'It's probably all OK, I'll just give it a quick check.' That mindset isn't conducive to productive checking. Say instead, 'There are bound to be some errors here and it's my job to find them so that they get corrected before the book goes to print.' The most important point is to read what you have actually written – what is there on the page – rather than what you think you have written. As well as double-spacing, use a large enough font. Use methods designed to slow down the reading so that you don't, as it were, get ahead of yourself. You might try reading aloud, for example, or moving a ruler gradually down the page.

There are two basic approaches to checking and it is worth using both in turn. First, there is the holistic method. You read the text as a whole, in the order in which you have written it. You read as vigilantly as possible and mark any problems that you uncover, whatever they may be. They might be of several different sorts: the misspelling of a name; a word missing from a sentence; a table or figure missing; an ambiguous sentence or one that doesn't quite say what you wanted it to say; a missing apostrophe; an inaccurate cross-reference; statistics that don't tally; a decimal point in the wrong place; an incomplete caption or quotation; and so on. Regardless of the problem, you first mark it and then put it right.

The second method is analytical. You select certain features that you wish to focus on. When establishing your checklist, include a range of items. Ensure that, between them, they are helping you to check that the text is (a) complete, (b) consistent, and (c) accurate. For example, when checking for completeness, focus on internal references. If, for example, you have referred your reader to 'fig. 3.3', you need now to ensure that the figure is indeed there and correctly numbered. When checking for consistency, ask yourself what policies you have adopted concerning such matters as nomenclature, transcription, measurement, labelling, and so on. Over the course of several months' writing, it is very easy to change policies without realising, especially if you have cut and pasted from texts written on other occasions. When checking for accuracy, concentrate on all those points that reviewers pounce on so gleefully: unfaithful quotations, incorrect dates, statistics that don't add up, references with the wrong publication dates, and so on.

Remember that an important criterion for accuracy is conformity with whatever style guide has been specified by your publishers. A reference, for example, might be bibliographically accurate, yet fail to conform to the publishers' preferred style. Similarly, the text may include spellings that are supported by your dictionary or spell-checker but fail to conform to the style guide. Opinions vary between authors on the question of when one should begin to worry about this. I used to ignore the style guide entirely until late in the writing process, on the basis that I didn't want pedantic points (whether inverted commas should be single or double, for example) to interfere with the process of composition. But then, when it came to checking, I would start to regret that policy, since the corrections always took longer than I'd envisaged. Now I try to internalise some of the key features of the guide so that I can get them right from the start. As I say, opinions vary.

PRESENTATION

The final process before your typescript is ready to deliver concerns presentation. Here again it is the writer's secretarial skills that are foremost. Your publishers will have specified how they wish the text to be formatted. The specification is likely to include such matters as:

- Word-processing package
- Font
- Line-spacing
- Page size and margins
- Pagination

In addition, there will be instructions on how to present figures.

A few authors I have worked with have claimed to find the presentation process satisfying. Following the mechanical processes involved can (they tell me) be therapeutic. I am glad for them. Most authors just find it boring. It is, however, something that you can get 100 per cent right (and probably the only part of the writing process of which that can be said). If, for example, your publishers specify that the text must be double-spaced throughout, you can ensure that it is.

Getting the presentation stage right is more important than it sounds. Carelessness in presentation influences editors' perceptions, perhaps disproportionately. To see why, try the following mental experiment. An editor receive two typescripts (A and B) on the same day. (A) is dull and uninspired, but immaculately presented. (B) is written with flair and grace, yet the presentation is careless and fails to conform with the publishers' specification. For example, the author has included box lines in the text despite being asked not to. Or the editor finds that, although the body text has been double-spaced, text within tables hasn't been. (A) can be passed on for copy-editing straightaway. (B) involves a good deal of work in the editorial office before it can be passed for copy-editing. The question is, which aspect of (B) does the editor remember: the flair and the grace or the fact that it required several hours' work? And which typescript does the editor think more highly of? And which author does the editor wish to work with again?

OVERVIEW

This chapter, together with the previous one, has presented an account of writing seen as a process as opposed to a product. This account has traced half a dozen processes in sequence, namely: incubation; planning and preparation; drafting; redrafting; checking; and presentation. Before closing this account I would like to reiterate two points that I made at the beginning of Chapter 5:

1. authors are diverse, in terms both of what processes they use and of what works best for them;
2. the six-point model that we have used here is very much that – a model, designed to provide a somewhat simplified picture of reality.

In practice, authorial processes are messier than the above account implies. In particular, the sequence of processes is apt to follow a less orderly path. Obviously, some aspects of that sequence are logically necessary: you can only check text that has already been drafted, for example; similarly, you can only prepare to write something that has not yet been drafted. But the processes that we have examined one by one do commonly overlap. One might well start to redraft before one has finished drafting, for example. One might do some of the checking as one goes along.

The processes not only overlap: they are also recursive. Working on one process often sends one back to an earlier process in order to change it. For example, new ideas arrive whilst you are drafting your text; you realise that your original plan needs to be modified, so you return to it and rethink it. Writing frequently involves this kind of movement to and fro.

I hope, therefore, that whichever process you happen to be involved with at the time, you will find it useful to turn to the relevant part of the account that I have provided in these two chapters. And I hope too that if you find your movement between the various processes of writing to be less neat and orderly than my account, that will not concern you. In writing processes, orderliness and neatness do occur, but they are not the rule. Indeed, the only rule is what works.

SUMMARY

1. Writing a text is like negotiating a maze – specifically, a multi-centred turf maze.
2. Anticipate, the way trained sheepdogs anticipate.
3. When redrafting your writing, consider how to (a) reduce the text, (b) add to it, and (c) change it around. You may need to review it carefully before deciding which of these operations to perform.
4. Exploit your best ideas to the full.
5. When thinking about how to reduce or add to your text, think on both the macro and the micro scale.
6. When considering how to change text around, review (a) conceptual content, (b) lexis, (c) sentence structure, (d) discourse structure, and (e) context.
7. Check for completeness, consistency, and accuracy.
8. When it comes to presentation, perfection is possible and desirable.

CHAPTER 7

Craft

This chapter differs in texture from those that have preceded it. It is more fine-grained. It is concerned with the textual aspects of writing – the nitty-gritty, if you like. And it analyses the handling of text in a number of examples of academic works. At one level, the chapter is a rag bag. It covers topics as disparate as:

- paragraph openings
- tone
- tables and figures
- notes

However, there is a unifying concern. Each topic relates to one problem or another that is frequently encountered in academic texts, is fairly readily fixed, and has a considerable impact on the effectiveness of a piece of writing. The chapter as a whole is intended to provide a mini-toolkit for academic authorship, especially when it comes to redrafting one's text.

Before we begin to use the kit, however, let's consider what it is we are trying to achieve in academic writing. Writers do not always agree on what constitutes good writing. Different ideals apply to different kinds of texts. Travel writing may aim to be evocative, detective fiction to be suspenseful, cook books to be practical, and so on. Fortunately, however, when it comes to academic writing, there is a reasonable degree of consensus. Most academics, whether writers or readers, would agree that academic writing should usually aim to be:

- clear
- concise
- coherent

This list is not exhaustive. An academic text may aim to be other things as well (for example, informative or original or provocative), but the above three may be treated as essential. That is, an absence of clarity, concision or coherence would usually be seen as a Bad Thing.

Now let's turn to the toolkit.

PARAGRAPH OPENINGS

No doubt all parts of a text are important, but the opening sentences of paragraphs are particularly so. They may fulfil a number of functions, including the following:

1. providing content (opening sentences say something, just like any other sentence);
2. indicating (whether explicitly or implicitly) what the paragraph ahead is for or about;
3. providing a link (explicitly or implicitly) with the previous paragraph.

Often an opening sentence of a paragraph will do more than one of these at a time. Think of the opening sentences of paragraphs as the vertebrae that form the backbone of your text. It provides the structure that holds the body of your text together. If the backbone is strong, the text will be able to support itself.

Sometimes I find myself looking at some text I have drafted and thinking, 'This is a mess. It's all over the place. It needs sorting out.' This can be dispiriting: where on earth to begin? The answer is often to begin with the opening sentences of paragraphs. I find that, if I work through the text, making the opening sentence of each paragraph as tight as possible, it then becomes clear how to edit the rest of the prose.

As a first step, take a piece of your writing and try highlighting the opening sentence of each paragraph. Then read through the text, reading only the sentences that you have highlighted. Ask yourself, 'How much sense does the text make from these sentences alone?' The answer will provide an indication of the strength of the backbone of your text.

Let us consider some sample text. The text in the box below has been created from the opening sentences of the first ten paragraphs of a chapter called 'The Romantic Movement' in Bertrand Russell's *History of Western Philosophy*. (The Rousseau referred to is the French philosopher, Jean Jacques Rousseau (1712–78)). I have numbered the paragraphs.

How well does this writing measure up to our tests? The text inevitably feels jumpy. A few sentences – (5), for example – seem rather adrift. Yet the reader can make some sense of the text. The ride might be a bit bumpy, but we can stay on board. We are helped by the frequent positioning of the subject (S) and verb (V) early in the sentence: 'The romantic movement (S) was (V)'; 'Rousseau (S) appealed (V)'.

Overall, there is a good deal of coherence. One senses that there are underlying themes that bind the text together – a concern to trace

---

Box 7.1 Paragraph openings from Bertrand Russell, 'The Romantic Movement'

1. From the latter part of the eighteenth century to the present day, art and literature and philosophy, and even politics, have been influenced, positively or negatively, by a way of feeling which was characteristic of what, in a large sense, may be called the romantic movement.

2. The romantic movement was not, in its beginnings, connected with philosophy, though it came before long to have connections with it.

3. The first great figure in the movement is Rousseau, but to some extent he only expressed already existing tendencies.

4. Rousseau appealed to the already existing cult of sensibility, and gave it a breadth and scope that it might not otherwise have possessed.

5. The romantics were not without morals; on the contrary, their moral judgements were sharp and vehement.

6. By the time of Rousseau, many people had grown tired of safety, and begun to desire excitement.

7. The romantic movement is characterized, as a whole, by the substitution of aesthetic for utilitarian standards.

8. The temper of the romantics is best studied in fiction.

9. The romantic movement, in spite of owing its origin to Rousseau, was at first mainly German.

10. The beginnings of romanticism in England can be seen in the writings of the satirists.

the origins ('in its beginnings', 'The first great figure', 'By the time') and chart the geography (from Rousseau in France, to Germany, to England) of romanticism. These are themes that would enable one to discern at least something of the sequence of the original text, even if I had presented them in a jumbled order.

Now let's consider the functions of these sentences. In general, they fulfil the first of the functions we itemised above: that is, they provide content. One learns a good deal about romanticism from these sentences, even though they are divorced from the paragraphs they open. Many of them also serve to indicate what lies ahead in the text of the paragraph that follows. Paragraph (3), for example, proceeds to characterise the 'existing tendencies' mentioned in its opening sentence; (6) develops the theme of safety versus excitement; and (10) cites examples of satirists.

The sentences do not explicitly link to preceding paragraphs (there are no phrases such as 'A further example …' or 'This can also be seen …'). Nevertheless, there are some implicit links, provided in part by repetition of words ('Rousseau', in particular). There is, therefore, at least some sense of continuity.

I do not think these sentences are perfect: (1) seems rather fussy and convoluted. I do question Russell's use of sentences comprising two clauses joined by 'and'. This may, however, result from a desire to give the prose a sense of balance and rhythm. And the compound sentences are not unremitting. Single-clause sentences such as (8) and (10) help to keep the passage moving. Overall, therefore, it seems to me that the sentences are doing a lot of work. They are efficient and effective. Paragraph openings such as these do not guarantee that the rest of the text will be successful, but they certainly make success likely. The backbone of the prose is strong.

There is a danger in using an unusually talented author like Russell as a model or a standard. We can't all be Bertrand Russells. Moreover, there is a question of genre. Russell was writing what we now call a crossover text. In aiming at a popular market, he had to be sure to write lucidly, without jargon; but he was also free to write without the encumbrance of scholarly references and nuances.

To balance this account, therefore, let's look at a sample of text from a contemporary monograph. *Widening Participation in Post-Compulsory Education* by Liz Thomas deals with the question of how to ensure that more students continue their education (at college or university) beyond their years of schooling. I think it's a good book when judged by the ideals identified above, namely clarity, conciseness, and coherence. The box below summarises the first half of Chapter 4 of the book by including (a) the headings and (b) the opening sentence of each paragraph. For the sake of clarity I have added labels in square brackets and have numbered the paragraphs.

Box 7.2 Opening sentences from first half of Chapter 4 of Liz Thomas, *Widening Participation in Post-Compulsory Education*

[chapter title] **The Labour Market and Participation in Post-Compulsory Education and Training**

[heading] INTRODUCTION

1. In addition to the impacts of the education sector, the labour market can impinge upon participation in post-compulsory education and training in a number of ways.
2. First, this chapter considers the role of labour market opportunities that help to determine the other options available to potential students, in particular, what sort of job they can get if they choose not to go into full time education or training.
3. Second, this chapter turns to the impact of labour market opportunities and job security that contribute significantly to the income available to 'invest' in education and training.
4. Finally, this chapter considers the influence of rates of return from the labour market on participation in post-compulsory education, as this determines the economic rate of return on 'investments' in learning.

[heading] THE OPPORTUNITY COST OF POST-COMPULSORY EDUCATION

5. The opportunity cost of any course of action refers to what is forgone.
6. In the UK, young people first have a choice regarding whether to continue in education or to enter the labour market at the age of 16.
7. Empirical research shows that the availability of opportunities in the labour market and in the education sector are both highly likely to influence people's decisions.

Box 7.2 (*Cont.*)

8. Michael Banks and colleagues report that while they were conducting research in the mid-1980s about young people growing up in the UK, two significant changes took place.
9. Similar trends can be seen amongst mature students during times of economic decline.
10. A closely related issue for the mature students involved in this research was the availability of benefits.
11. In general, it can be surmised that one impact of high unemployment is greater participation in post-compulsory education and training, although this may be offset to some extent by financial constraints.
12. It is debatable, however, whether or not employment training schemes should be classified as 'training' (on a par with vocational education), or whether they should more accurately be described as a (poor) substitute for employment, and a means of gaining access to cheap labour by employers.
13. During periods of high unemployment both governments and students are not only attracted to training and vocationally oriented education, but also towards higher education.
14. It can be concluded that the opportunity cost of education, which is determined, at least in part, by the labour market, influences decisions about participation in both education and training, although it is not the only factor influencing demand for education.

These sentences certainly provide content. One learns a substantial amount about the relationship between the labour market and the education sector from these sentences alone. Often they also signal clearly what the remainder of the paragraph will deal with. For example, paragraph (5) develops and applies the concept of 'opportunity cost'; (8) details the findings from the research project cited in the opening sentence; whilst (10) provides an account of social security benefit payments. Thomas also provides a sense of cohesion by constructing sentences that relate back to preceding paragraphs. The simple device of 'first … second … finally' shows that paragraphs (2), (3), and (4) contribute to the same argument; phrases such as 'similar trends' and 'closely related issue' make links between paragraphs explicit; whilst phrases such as 'in general' and 'it can be concluded' signal a pulling together of the argument.

The writing is, of course, far from perfect. One might argue that some of the devices that we have just identified are somewhat clunky. Perhaps the handling of adverbs ('highly', 'closely') is a little awkward. Some authors would take issue with Thomas's use of the passive voice as the default mode for the chapter (though my own view is that, for the most part, she carries it off well). Beginning a paragraph with a citation, as Thomas does in (8), rarely makes for cohesion. Some sentences – notably (12) – perhaps try to do too much – though the effect is leavened by the regular use of straightforward, single clause, sentences, notably (5) and (9).

Overall, however, the writing meets all three of our ideals – clarity, conciseness, and coherence – pretty well. Perhaps there are even places where the writing is *too* concise: in places a more relaxed construction, with longer sentences such as (12) split into shorter, simpler sentences, might help. One could make the writing more felicitous, but would the gain be so very great? Though Thomas might lack the natural lucidity of a Bertrand Russell (though she seems better than Russell at linking back to preceding paragraphs), the prose works. One learns a good deal about the subject, and the author's argument, without the text making things difficult for us. The backbone of the writing is certainly sufficiently strong for its purpose.

Precisely because she is a good, rather than great, author, Thomas may in fact be a better model than Russell for aspiring authors. Trying to write a monograph in the rhythmical, balanced, nicely turned style of a Bertrand Russell might prove a dispiriting experience. The virtues of Thomas's style seem more achievable.

TONE

The tone of a piece of writing is important. It is something that we sense and, often, react to. Yet it can be difficult to get a handle on. What exactly is it?

The most useful definition of tone is, I think, that provided by I. A. Richards: 'The speaker has ordinarily *an attitude to his listener*. He chooses or arranges his words differently as his audience varies, in automatic or deliberate *recognition of his relation to them*. The tone of his utterance reflects his awareness of this relation, his sense of how he stands towards those he is addressing.' Richards's conception of tone as something that links language to relationship is, I think, spot on.

We can apply this conception to help change the tone of a piece. To facilitate this, we will take Richards's notion of a 'relationship' between speaker and listener and analyse it into two components. One component consists of status. When reviewing a piece of draft text, one may ask: does the speaker (i.e. writer) talk up to the listener (i.e. reader), talk down, or on a level? The second component is distance: one may ask, does the speaker seem close to the reader or far away?

We may think of this model in terms of a graph (Figure 7.1). For example, a piece of writing in which the author seemed to talk down to the reader and from a distance, would be located towards the top right of the above graph.

Locating a sample of text on the above graph helps to show how the tone may be modified. Consider, for example, the following samples. Text (A) is a passage from near the start of a chapter on socialisation in a text called *Sports in Society* by Jay Coakley (an American sociology professor). Text (B) is taken from the opening of a chapter on sport psychology in a textbook called *Sports Training Principles* by Frank Dick (an eminent British sports coach).

(A) Socialization is an active process of learning and social develop-
    ment, which occurs as we interact with one another and become
    acquainted with the social world in which we live. It involves
    the formation of ideas about who we are and what is important
    in our lives. We are *not* simply passive learners in the socializa-
    tion process. We actively participate in our own socialization as
    we influence those who influence us. We actively interpret what
    we see and hear, and we accept, resist, or revise the messages we
    receive about who we are, about the world, and about what we
    should do as we make our way in the world. Therefore, socializa-
    tion is not a one-way process of social influence through which
    we are molded and shaped. Instead, it is an interactive proc-
    ess through which we actively connect with others, synthesize
    information, and *make decisions* that shape our own lives and
    the social world around us.

    This definition of *socialization*, which I use to guide my
    research, is based on a combination of *critical* and *interaction-
    ist* approaches. Therefore, not all sociologists would agree with

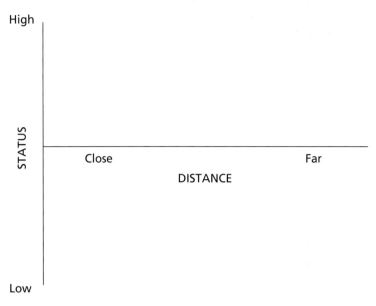

Fig. 7.1 Graphical analysis of the components of tone

it. Those using functionalist or conflict theory approaches, for example, would define *socialization* in slightly different terms. Their definitions have an impact on how they do research and the questions they ask about sports and socialization.

(B) The education of the athlete by the coach and supporting team of specialists, and the athlete's self-education thereafter, is an underoptimised if not underestimated aspect of training. Critical reflection, a coaching skill concerned with both the aims and consequences of technical efficiency accompanied by open enquiry guided by 'attitudes of open mindedness, responsibility, and whole-heartedness' (Pollard, 1988), reminds us that coaching does not take place in a social vacuum. Yet on a practical level, the coach receives more technical guidance than that which assists the comprehension of human interactions. As coaching has developed in scientific literacy, its fundamental humanistic social nature remains less understood. By virtue of this pattern, it is possible that less time is invested in what we are less familiar with. Consequently, the technical preparation of the performer is a stronger element than the preparation of the less visible, intangible aspects of performance. Technical literacy has appeared as a base-line coaching skill where coach-differentiating variables such as imagination, vision and risk-taking are rare (Murray, 1999). Whilst the science of sport psychology has physical indicators, such as biofeedback training, part of its attraction and inherent challenge is the non-quantifiable synergistic impact when intuitive and creative variables are optimised, resulting in the realisation of true athletic potential.

The coach has two main responsibilities: to prepare the athlete physically and technically *for* the sport, and to develop 'the athlete socially and ethically *through* the sport'. This begins with sensitising the athlete via self-awareness.

The passages are performing comparable jobs – introducing the reader to the application of principles from behavioural science to sport – yet the treatment is clearly very different (almost comically so). The contrast between the two passages involves more than just tone, but tone is certainly an important factor.

Let us try to analyse the tone of each passage. On training courses I have asked scores of prospective academic authors to plot these passages on the above graph and the results have indicated a good deal of consensus. First, let us consider distance. Participants usually locate Passage (A) towards the left-hand side of the graph. It isn't intimate, but – certainly compared to most academic texts – it is warm and friendly. The use of the first person ('who we are … our own lives … I use … my research') seems to bring the voice up close, as if we were in a room together. The passage is usually located in the top half of the graph. The writer certainly wants to instruct us and does so confidently ('Therefore, socialization is not a one-way process of social influence'). He thus positions himself above us. But he does not seem to do so very much, especially compared to many pedagogical texts. He reminds us that his views are debatable ('not all sociologists would agree') and, amidst the academic-ese ('a combination of *critical* and *interactionist* approaches'), he weaves in a good deal of homely language ('who we are and what is important in our lives'). Overall, I have heard the tone in this passage described as a democratic one, which seems to me apt.

Now let's consider Passage (B). The voice here seems much more distant – a function of the impersonal third person and the passive voice ('The education of the athlete by the coach') and the very literary, polysyllabic style far removed from the speaking voice (try reading aloud, for example, the first sentence or that beginning 'Whilst the science of sport psychology …') This text should therefore be placed towards the right-hand side of our graph.

Now consider the second dimension, i.e. status. Again, the writer positions himself above us. He is very definitely instructing us – and he does so assertively: 'The coach has two main responsibilities … This begins with sensitising the athlete via self-awareness' – there is no room for debate here. Most participants on my courses also react to the heavily Latinate diction ('underoptimised if not underestimated') and cite it as a reason (Latin being historically the language of the elite) for feeling that the author is talking down to us. The passage should be located nearer to the top of the graph than Passage (A). I have heard the tone of Passage (B) described as 'authoritarian', but that seems to me unwarranted: 'authoritative' would perhaps be more apt. Figure 7.2 attempts to show the relative positions of the two passages.

Having used the graph to pin down the tone of each passage, we can readily set about revising the tone. Suppose, for example, we wished to move Passage (B) down the graph by making the relationship between writer and reader less unequal in status. We might remove that 'underoptimised' by replacing the construction 'The education of the athlete … is an underoptimised … aspect' with something like 'In general, coaches could make more use of education …'. We might make the syntax less assertive too. For example, instead of 'This begins with sensitising the athlete via self-awareness', we might write something like 'One way to begin …'. Now suppose we wish to move the same passage towards the left, i.e. to make the tone less distant. We could try making the language less literary. For example, we could simply omit the word 'thereafter'; and replace 'By virtue of this pattern, it is possible that' with 'Perhaps'.

The combined effect of these changes is to move Passage (B) in the direction of Passage (A). It would take quite a lot to actually move it all the way – but nevertheless we can see that even quite small tweaks have an effect. That is good news when it comes to revising our own drafts. May I invite you now to decide what you would do to move

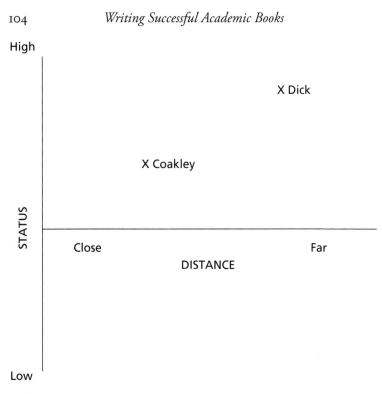

Fig. 7.2 Graphical analysis of tone in (A) Coakley and (B) Dick

Passage (B) in the direction of Passage (A)? How much work would be required to get the two passages, originally so distinct, to meet each other on the graph?

Note that my concern here has not been to express a preference for one tone over another. Though in my experience most readers prefer the tone of Passage (A), some feel it is too informal and others feel that it would be appropriate only for a textbook – that a monograph would require a tone somewhat closer to that of (B). My concern here, however, is to illustrate what tone consists of and how (readily) it may be adjusted.

TABLES AND FIGURES

Tables and figures are staple components of academic writing, especially in the sciences. Yet, especially in authors' drafts, they frequently give rise to difficulty. However, many of the problems associated with figures and tables are easily soluble. The solutions usually come from putting oneself in the shoes of the reader. Let's consider each problem in turn. I should explain that I have tended to talk about tables and figures together because, though they are different things, many of the problems associated with them apply to both.

The first problem is that tables and figures are often not properly introduced. We are reading though a text, we reach the end of a paragraph, and then WHAM! – we bump up against a table or a figure. 'What's this?' we wonder. The moral is: tell your reader what is coming up (for example, 'Figure 1.1 shows …').

The second problem is that the table or figure may not be positioned in the most helpful place. Perhaps we are introduced to 'Figure 1.1', but it turns out to be several paragraphs away, perhaps over the page. Though often this is a function of typesetting (and may be unavoidable), it sometimes results from carelessness on the part of the author.

The third problem is that it may not be clear how to read the table or figure. One author I worked with, for example, devised a wonderful chart to explain the different approaches towards innovation taken by multinational enterprises. The figure aspired to a work of art – lots of intersecting arcs, variants of dotted lines, and so on. For the author, the figure summarised a good deal of careful thought. But, try as I might, I couldn't make head or tail of it. The moral is not to assume that the interpretation of a figure is self-evident: you may need to talk your reader through it. Moreover, be sure to provide a concise but informative caption.

The fourth problem is that the table or figure may not show what the author claims it does. One author I was working with recently provided a table of Russian economic statistics. Row 3, he assured the reader, showed how the telecommunications industry had grown faster than the economy as a whole. Row 3 in fact showed no such thing: it showed only the performance of the telecommunications industry. To find information on the performance of the Russian economy I had to read Row 1. To find the relationship between the two sets of data (i.e. for the telecommunications industry and for the Russian economy), I needed a calculator. What was needed was an additional row showing the divergence between the two sets of figures. A more extreme case is when the figures in fact show the very opposite of what the text claims. One author I published included in his typescript a table showing, according to the text, that certain ethnic minorities performed less well than the general population in school examinations. What the table in fact revealed was that the groups in question performed *above* average. The moral is to put oneself in the shoes of a sceptical and not particularly generous reader and see where the cracks begin to show.

The fifth problem is that a table or figure might show too much. The table of Russian economic statistics to which I refer above in fact contained seven rows of data. Most of them were never mentioned in the text and, so far as I can see, were wholly irrelevant. The effect of the extraneous data was simply to distract the reader and cause uncertainty ('What is all this for?' the reader asks, 'Am I missing something?'). This situation tends to arise when an author has simply cut and pasted a table or figure in total from another source, rather than editing it. The moral is to provide the reader with all of the information required but nothing that is superfluous.

The above list of problems associated with tables and figures is by no means exhaustive. It does, however, capture the problems that occur most frequently. Below is a checklist designed to help you identify potential problems in your own writing.

1. Is the table or figure appropriately (a) numbered and (b) captioned?
2. Does the main text refer to it? Does the text make the purpose of the table or figure clear?
3. Is the table or figure optimally positioned relative to the text?
4. Is it clear how it should be read/interpreted? What guidance does the reader require?
5. Is it complete?
6. Have you removed unnecessary/irrelevant content?

NOTES

The handling of notes – footnotes or endnotes – is also a common source of problems. Notes force readers literally to take their eye off the main text. They can be extremely irritating, especially when used excessively. There are good reasons for using notes. In particular, they are useful as a way of identifying sources without having to clutter the main text. They may also be useful for providing technical information about those sources – about questions of translation, for example, or the integrity of data. Often, though, notes are used to do no such thing. Rather, they are used as a half-way house. One cannot decide how important a certain point is: should it be included in the main text or omitted? The temptation is to compromise and dump it in the notes – half-in, half-out, as it were. This is simply lazy authorship. The solution is to work through one's notes when redrafting text and allocate each one (bar those dealing with sources) into one of two categories: those that need to be incorporated into the main text and those that need to be omitted altogether. Your reader will have cause to thank you.

SUMMARY

1. The ideals of clarity, concision, and coherence are central to academic writing.
2. The opening sentences of paragraphs are like vertebrae: make the spine of your text as strong as possible.
3. Tone is a function of the relationship between writer and reader.
4. Often a few tweaks can do much to adjust the tone of a passage.
5. Tables and figures need to be introduced and helpfully positioned.
6. It needs to be clear to the reader how and why tables and figures should be read.
7. Ensure that tables and graphs show what you claim they show and do not include extraneous data.
8. When you redraft your text, seek to get rid of notes by incorporating them into your main text or omitting them altogether.

CHAPTER 8

Dissertations

'Can I turn my dissertation into a book? And if so, how?' are questions that acquisitions editors are often asked by doctoral graduates. Since virtually all of the dissertations that get published in book form do so as monographs, these questions are essentially about a particular section of the monograph market. In Part 1 above, this book considered the monograph market in general and took a rather bullish view of it. In the special case of monographs based on dissertations, however, a more nuanced view is called for.

First, let's consider the context. This in fact varies hugely between disciplines. In some disciplines there is little call for monographs, whilst in others the market is strong. Generally, Humanities, Arts, and Social Science subjects tend to be more hospitable to monographs than do 'STEM' (i.e. scientific, technical, engineering, and medical) disciplines. There is also a strong monograph market in professional subjects (tourism management, for example), not least because business school libraries and professionals in the corporate sector provide additional markets.

The context for monographs also varies between territories. In the German-speaking world, for example, there is a tradition of publishing books based directly on research dissertations. Though not perhaps as robust as it once was, the tradition remains strong, not least because monograph authorship still functions to some extent as a passport for obtaining tenure. Imprints specialising in such publications remain an important part of the Germanic publishing landscape.

In Anglophone territories the position is more fragmented. Though the monograph market as a whole may be in good health, the publication of books based on doctoral dissertations plays an ever smaller role within it. Moreover, the phrase 'based on' is likely to apply rather loosely here, since when such dissertations do lead on to book publications they are likely to undergo (as we will see) quite a transformation in the process.

Notice here the significance of the word 'book'. Doctoral dissertations do in fact get published (in the sense of 'made public') readily and regularly in the Anglophone world, though not in book form. Commercial services have developed for selling dissertations online – most notably ProQuest's UMI Dissertation Express, which at the time of writing offers nearly 2 million graduate texts. In addition, many universities have established repositories for graduate dissertations.

Naturally, this has had a direct impact on the market for monographs derived from dissertations. Libraries can see no reason to use scarce funds to purchase dissertations in book form if the dissertations themselves are readily available already. Libraries will only purchase books that clearly provide some added value. Monographs need therefore to be different from, and in some sense better than, the dissertations from which they derive.

We need, therefore, to consider how monographs may be distinguished from dissertations. To do this we will focus on three major aspects, namely readership, purpose, and structure. Let's take dissertations first. Most of these reach only a very limited readership. If you have written a doctoral thesis, your supervisor and the external examiner will – one trusts! – read it. A few other people close to the research situation may do so too. For most dissertations, only a handful of people in total will read the whole text.

Strangely, the dissertation, unlike other texts written for small groups (memos, for example), cannot be addressed to its actual readers. One cannot, for example, write the dissertation in the second person (e.g. 'your [i.e. the supervisor's] own journal article is pertinent here') or begin the dissertation 'Dear Dr [name of supervisor] and Dr [name of examiner]'. Instead, the dissertation has to be addressed to some implied reader, whose identity tends to be rather uncertain. (This uncertainty is one of the reasons why dissertations can be hard to write.) Often it would seem to be someone who is an expert in your field, though a pedantic and sceptical one.

Consider now the purpose of a dissertation. This is in fact twofold. First, it is to advance knowledge. What constitutes advancement of knowledge – and, indeed, a sufficient advancement to merit a doctorate – is of course a tricky epistemological question, though thankfully not one that needs to detain us here. All we need say here is that the examiners must be persuaded that they have grounds for crediting the dissertation with such advancement.

The second function of the dissertation is to gain the author a qualification. This function is more anthropological than epistemological. Conferring a doctorate is a rite of passage signalling completion of an apprenticeship and providing, at least potentially, a passport to a further career. To fulfil this function, the dissertation must provide evidence of industriousness, mastery of canonical research methods, and negotiation of disciplinary norms.

In a well-written dissertation, these two functions will tend to dovetail. A well-written literature review, for example, might reveal how the research grows out of the literature – how, for example, the review has been used to identify a problem that the research has then been designed to solve. This will fulfil the epistemological function. In doing so, it might indicate too that the author has covered lots of ground and put in a good number of hours in the library in the process (the anthropological function). Often, however, the two functions sit rather uneasily together. Part of the literature review genuinely informs the research; part of it consists merely of going through the ropes.

Now consider the structure of the dissertation. Dissertations – or, rather, the arguments contained within them – come in various shapes. In most dissertations, however, it is the conclusion that carries the biggest punch. This is the section that is designed to bring everything together, emphasise the most important findings and their implications, and say to the examiners, 'See, I deserve a doctorate!' In this sense (alone), dissertations are rather like those classic detective novels in which it is on the last page that the identity of the murderer is revealed. The ending clinches it.

Now consider, in contrast, monographs. It is difficult to know how many people actually read monographs. One can obtain sales figures (indicating that many monographs sell a few hundred copies), but these are only proxies for readership numbers: some copies may be purchased but left unread, whilst others (especially in the case of library copies) may be read by more than one person. Whatever the true figures may be, it is safe to say that on average a monograph will be read by many more people than a dissertation. It will also be read by a more diverse readership. Monographs are more likely to find readers working in other contexts, in other parts of the world, in different subject areas, and at different levels.

The function of a monograph will also differ from that of a dissertation. In a book, the emphasis will fall on the epistemological function rather than the anthropological. Typically, readers will seek to learn from the book, rather than to use it to assess the career credentials of the author. And, as a result, there needs to be an emphasis on communication: the author must seek not simply to establish some advance in knowledge but also to convey it effectively.

Dissertations and monographs differ in structure too. There is of course no reason why a monograph should not contain a powerful conclusion. But, precisely because nobody has to read a monograph, the author cannot rely on the reader's willingness to defer gratification. Life is too short for people to read books of a couple of hundred pages in the hope that the ending will show our investment of effort to have been worthwhile.

In a monograph, the opening chapter needs to pack a punch. It needs to demonstrate beyond question that the book is worthy of the reader's attention. Journalists are taught to include the most important points at the top of a story. In this structural sense, a monograph is more like a newspaper article than a whodunit.

There are, then, fundamental differences between dissertations and monographs in terms of readership, function, and structure. What are the implications for the doctoral graduate posing the questions with which we began this chapter: 'Can I turn my dissertation into a book? And if so, how?'

Here we should consider three possible scenarios. The first is not to proceed from dissertation to book. Put your dissertation behind you. Leave it on the shelf. Go on to something new. From a negative point of view, you may well have become bored with your dissertation. Some doctoral graduates view the prospect of doing yet more work on their dissertation rather like a prisoner would view the prospect of an extended sentence. More positively, your doctoral research may have thrown up new questions and opportunities that you are eager to explore.

I don't seem to come across authors who, having chosen to leave the dissertation behind, come to regret their decision. I recognise, however, that this choice is not always an option. If your goal is to obtain tenure, you work in a system where publication of a monograph is regarded as a prerequisite for that, and you can see no other way of producing such a book, then seeking to convert your dissertation into a book is clearly essential. This brings us to the two alternative scenarios.

The second scenario is the minimalist approach. You have a dissertation; you want to get a monograph published; dissertations and monographs tend to be approximately equal in length: so you ask yourself, 'What is the least I have to do to turn the one into the other?' You recognise that, in the process of moving from dissertation to book, something has to change, but aim to ensure that 'something' is as little as possible.

This approach is not a healthy one. It produces a quick-fix mentality that goes something like this:

1. either move the methodology chapter to an appendix at the back of the book or take it out altogether;
2. slim down the literature review to the salient points;
3. reduce the endnotes and references as far as possible without having to do much rewriting as a result.

These are probably all moves in the right direction. But they are not enough. They do not produce the added value that makes the book marketable. There may be commissioning editors who are happy to work with authors who adopt this approach – but I haven't met them yet. And from the author's point of view, it is a joyless, uncreative way to work.

The third scenario involves starting from the other end. That is, one starts by thinking about the book. What kind of book is required? What does a good book on this subject need? Having decided on the desiderata, you can then turn to your dissertation and consider how to use it as a resource. The question 'How can I quarry my dissertation to produce some of the material I need for the book that needs to be written?' produces quite different results from 'What's the least I have to do to get from A to B?'

How, then, should you proceed if you have decided that you wish to move from dissertation to book? First, after finishing your dissertation, allow as much time to elapse as you can afford before starting work on the book project. Even if the clock is ticking for applications for tenured jobs, a break – however small – between the two projects will help you to steer clear of the quick-fix mentality.

Use the time to study other monographs to help you decide what makes for success in the genre. Consider monographs away from your specialism and even outside your discipline. This will help to focus attention on matters such as form, style, and tone rather than content.

Above all, make use of the many excellent resources available. It is deeply frustrating that, on the one hand, there are a great many doctoral graduates wanting to know how to progress from dissertation to book and, on the other, there are a number of excellent, readily available, resources on the subject – yet the two rarely seem to meet. If this chapter results in more prospective authors making use of these resources, it will certainly have served a useful purpose. The resources (more fully described in the notes to this chapter) include: William Germano, *From Dissertation to Book*; a collection edited by Eleanor Harman and others, entitled *The Thesis and the Book*; and a collection, edited by Beth Luey, called *Revising Your Dissertation*. None of them is a long or difficult read.

The advice given in Chapter 3, concerning the selection of publishers and submission of a book proposal, applies as much in this context as any other. You are likely to be asked to submit a sample chapter.

When you are drafting your proposal and sample chapter, decide as early in the process as possible on your target reader. Doing so will, in effect, yield criteria for making the judgements required. I wholeheartedly endorse some advice given by Germano: think of your reader as someone intelligent and well educated, but not necessarily learned in your subject.

When you come to examine your dissertation as a resource for your monograph, consider what needs to be (a) reduced or omitted, (b) added, (c) changed, or (d) deliberated upon. The following plan follows this schema.

Reducing or omitting

1. Be tough on methodological material. The purpose of the book, remember, isn't to demonstrate your credentials for a doctorate. You may be able to omit methodological discussion entirely. If there are some aspects of your methodology that genuinely need to be discussed – say, because the reader won't be able to understand the findings without it – seek to integrate the discussion into the discourse as a whole, rather than devoting a whole chapter to it. If you have made an important methodological innovation, that is probably better explained in a journal paper devoted to the topic rather than as part of your monograph. It is likely to be the substantive aspects of your research that readers of your book want to hear about.

2. Be tough too on your review of the literature. It is likely that you will want to relate your book to previous work in the field. In doing so, however, focus on the fact that the point is to help your reader by providing some bearings (and, again, not to establish your doctoral credentials). Concentrate on situating your study in relation to the most salient works in the field: don't provide an exhaustive account.

3. Follow the advice in Chapter 7 above concerning notes (pp. 106–7).

4. Delete inessential references (please!). You may find this difficult to do. You may have spent the last few years of your life straining to get as many references as possible into your work. That, however, was largely the result of what we have called the anthropological function of your dissertation. As a reader of books, my heart always sinks when I see a page littered with references – sometimes, it seems, multiple references at the end of every sentence. It just looks messy, like potholes in the street. I always want to ask reference-happy authors, what do you expect me to *do* with all these references? One particular kind of reference that I invariably find fatuous is what I call a 'global' reference: the author writes a sentence, making a point of their own, and then in parenthesis at the end of the sentence provides a reference to one or more entire works. And that is all – no explanation is given. Does the writer seriously suppose that I will head off to the library and read a few hundred pages of some other work in the hope of identifying the link? And

what would I do with it, if and when I found it? Please, include only those references that are essential.

5. Similarly, restrict your bibliography. I frequently see monographs with bibliographies extending to dozens of pages. What is the point? I always want to say to the authors concerned, 'I have Internet access, you know.'

6. Seek to exclude raw data. Many dissertations include extensive data, much of it unprocessed. When I studied Mathematics, my teacher used to demand that I should 'show my working', i.e. show not only the answer I got to in the end but also how I got there. Many postgraduates find themselves in the same position. But writing a book is a different ball game. Academic research may be a fascinating activity, but a spectator sport it is not. You can save the reader the raw data and provide a single-sentence reference to the archive instead.

Adding

Earlier, I recommended, following Germano, that you should establish as your target reader someone who is not learned in your own field. That makes the reader very different from your supervisor or examiner. It means that you will have to add material. Your new readership will require more context. They may ask similar questions to your examiner: where does this study come in the scheme of things, what is the point of it, why is it needed? – and so on. The answers you provide, however, will need to be very different from those you gave in your viva. They will need to be very much broader and they will need to take less for granted. Things that may be taken for granted between specialists – central concepts, well-established schools of thought, and so on – may be entirely new to the readers of your book. You will need, therefore, to spend more time covering the basics.

This type of writing can be fun. If you enjoy teaching, the task of welcoming new readers to your field and guiding them through it will appeal to you. And if you have experience of teaching students, you will be able to draw on that experience in order to help you pitch your explanations appropriately. It can also be refreshing to revisit the basics in your subject and concentrate on getting them just right. And it usually isn't taxing to do.

Changing

You need to change your use of jargon – both the way you use it and the extent. Dissertations inevitably contain much jargon. Many postgraduates actually look for opportunities to drop jargon into their dissertations. Jargonifying the text, they reason, is one of the ways of showing that it fulfils the anthropological function: it indicates that the author has joined the disciplinary community.

Book authorship requires a move in the opposite direction. Whenever jargon can be replaced by plain language, it should be. Whenever it is unavoidable – jargon sometimes is genuinely useful – it needs to be explained to the reader when it is introduced. This may include formal definitions and even, especially if jargon takes the form of acronyms, a glossary.

The major change that is required, however, is structural. As we saw above, books require a different shape from that of a dissertation. I said then that books need to be structured less like whodunits and more like newspaper stories. I recently asked one specialist monograph editor what piece of advice – if she could give just one – she would give prospective authors. 'Write a cracking good opening chapter', was her reply. It is difficult to argue with that.

William Germano recommends writing an opening chapter that could stand as an essay in its own right. That seems to me difficult to achieve, but a worthy aim. Such a chapter is valuable in its own right: it also becomes a candidate for anthologising in readers or course packs and is likely to gain citations for the author.

Deliberating

The question of what style you should use for your dissertation is a major one. Precisely because dissertations tend to be addressed to an ill-defined or even illusory implied reader, they tend to be written in a formal, impersonal, style. With books, however, a wider range of styles is permissible. This requires the author to make some decisions about style and tone.

Whenever a group of prospective authors gather to discuss academic authorship, questions concerning grammatical person (first, third, or both?) and active versus passive constructions are likely to arise. There are no easy answers to these questions. They depend in part on disciplinary norms. If you are writing ethnography, your writing may well be characterised by free use of the first person; if you are writing hard science, it won't (though Watson and Crick's famous paper on DNA began, 'We wish to suggest …').

There are also differences between genres. Monographs, with which we are concerned here, will tend to use a more formal style than, say, student guides or how-to books (which may even make frequent use of the second person). That said, authors will usually adopt a less austere style for monographs than they would when writing journal papers. This is in part a function of length: 25 pages of formal text is tolerable; 250 pages, less so. Readers are likely to forgive a desire on your part to relax a bit, and, indeed, to welcome it. To ask readers to spend many hours with a text that offers no sense of personal voice or warmth is to risk seeming impolite.

A further variable is time. Fashions change. Take, for example, the dictum that scientific writing should be characterised by passive constructions. I meet some people who regard it as unquestionably correct and would feel that to do otherwise would be akin to showing their underwear in public. And I meet other people who regard it with mere amusement.

My own view is that this is a no-win situation – whichever policy you pursue, there will be somebody who doesn't like it – and, for precisely that reason, one that is not worth agonising about. One solution is imitation: ask yourself which authors in your discipline you most wish to be likened to – and then adopt their policies. Beyond that I suggest letting your fingers do the talking – start typing and go with the style that enables you to actually get the book written.

THE PUBLISHING CONTEXT REVISITED

At the start of this chapter, I said that the state of the market for books that derive from dissertations required a more nuanced account than that of monographs in general. Let us now revisit this issue. Many commentators see the lack of publishing opportunities for doctoral graduates as a further symptom of the supposed diseased state of academic publishing in general. Susan Bassnett is in no way idiosyncratic when, in the article I cited in Chapter 2, she writes: 'In the changed climate of reading, sales are often so absurdly low that many publishers have started taking a tough line with authors. Once, not so long ago, a postgraduate could expect to publish a good doctoral thesis, but today you have to advise your students to forget about a book and aim instead at a few articles.'

I do not concur with such laments. Though I would agree that the book-of-the-dissertation market is now very limited and probably still declining, I fail to see how this constitutes a backward step. We live in an age of digitalisation. That universities and electronic publishers have found new ways to archive and disseminate dissertations does not strike me as a cause for lamentation. Rather, it represents progress. And it frees publishing capital and library funds for the kinds of books you will want to write later in your career, long after your dissertation has been put to bed.

SUMMARY

1. If you don't *have* to turn your dissertation into a book, the best option might well be to move on to something new.
2. If you wish to transform your dissertation into a book, you must in the process add value.
3. Ask not 'What is the least work I have to do to revise the dissertation?' but rather, 'What would make a good book? What do I have to do to produce one?' – and then, 'How can I use my dissertation as a resource?'
4. Let the transformation between dissertation and book grow out of the differences between the two genres in terms of readership, function, and structure.
5. Write a new, cracking, opening chapter – preferably one that works as an essay in its own right.

Managing the Project

CHAPTER 9

Time

Part II of this book concentrated on the central aspect of the authorship, the writing itself. It focused closely on the generation and manipulation of text. Yet writing does not exist in a vacuum. Usually there are other people involved. And there are of course other things in our lives going on around our writing. Part III of this book, therefore, broadens the focus to take in some of these wider issues. This chapter focuses particularly on how to manage time as an author.

What principles can you use to allocate time to writing? You could rely on inspiration. You could just write when the mood takes you. Some books do get written like that. But it is a high-risk strategy – one most likely to result in you failing to write your book.

Alternatively, you could devise a schedule. Here it is helpful to draw on the advice provided by Eviatar Zerubavel in *The Clockwork Muse: A Practical Guide to Writing Theses, Dissertations, and Books.* Zerubavel (himself an academic author) recommends devising a schedule by dividing your week into various types of time. The key, he suggests is to begin by identifying those times of the week that, because of other claims on your time, you will not be able to devote to writing – and then to block off these times altogether. This seems to me a valuable suggestion. It establishes the need for realism from the start.

The second category of time is that best suited to writing. This is what Zerubavel calls 'A-time'. It is made up of times of the week when you are least likely to be interrupted. Zerubavel suggests – again I think rightly – that there are two kinds of opportunity here. There is the opportunity to find time – that is, to identify parts of the week where there is space between commitments. And there is the opportunity to create time. For some authors, this will involve periods late at night. More often, it is likely to be periods early in the morning, before the start of the usual working day.

We will in a moment consider how to make best use of A-time. But, first, let's briefly consider the final category of time. This is time – what Zerubavel calls 'B-time' – that is less than ideal for writing (mainly because of the likelihood of interruption) but which may nevertheless be of some use. These time slots, Zerubavel suggests, might 'be used for work that is directly related to your project yet requires less intense, focused concentration'. The particular example he gives is checking footnotes. There are, of course, many others. They include managing and backing up files, filling in gaps (that quotation that you want to include but couldn't find), and ordering books online from a library or bookstore.

I very much like Zerubavel's proposal to build B-time into the schedule. B-time activities do need to be done, yet authors frequently fail to allow time for them. Allocating time to them in the schedule not only ensures they get done, it also ensures that they don't eat into A-time – one of the most common causes of procrastination over writing.

Now let us return to A-time and consider how to optimise it. Some writing gurus suggest that there should be some A-time every day. That seems to me unrealistic – most of us have lifestyles that don't allow for quite such regularity. But I would certainly endorse the aim to schedule some A-time most days and also to try whenever possible to avoid consecutive blank days. If you achieve these two aims, writing will feel like something you do on a daily basis even if, strictly speaking, it isn't.

Many writing gurus suggest that you should set a very precise time for the start of a session. They also suggest that, when that time arrives, you should begin writing, by which they mean not preparing to write but actually generating text. If any preparation is needed, it should be done before the allotted time. I would certainly endorse both points. I suggest avoiding scheduling an A-time session to start either on the hour or on the half-hour. We tend to use phrases such as '11 o'clock' or 'half-ten' very loosely. It is all too easy for '11 o'clock' to stretch to, say, 11.10. If instead you say to yourself that you are going to start writing at 10.50 (or, even better, 10.48), you are far more likely to actually start promptly when the appointed time arrives. Such times might look a little odd in your diary, but they have the virtue of being unambiguous.

In *Becoming a Writer*, Dorothea Brande suggests that you should schedule your writing sessions for the same time each day. That is very good advice if you can manage it, since it is most likely to inculcate a habit of writing. But if your working or domestic life does not allow such a routine, there is no point agonising over it: simply writing on most days and always starting at an appointed time, even if that time varies from day to day, will also establish writing as a habit, though it may take a little longer to arrive at that point.

How long should you write for? It is impossible to generalise. Writing is a matter of rhythm, and rhythms vary greatly between authors. Jean Bolker, in *Writing Your Dissertation in Fifteen Minutes a Day: A Guide to Starting, Revising, and Finishing Your Doctoral Thesis*, suggests three ways of delimiting the session. First, there is what she calls the 'sit there' method: you designate a period of time during which you must stay in front of your screen or piece of paper and not go anywhere else – not even to make the coffee. Second, there is the 'inspiration method': you keep writing until you have come up with at least one or two decent ideas. Third, there is the 'many pages' method: you set yourself a defined number of pages and stop when, and only when, you have written them. Bolker recommends the third on the grounds that it rewards quick work: if you set yourself the task of writing six pages, then the quicker you write those pages, the sooner you can allow yourself to go and do something else. This seems to me fine if we are talking about writing in the sense of drafting, since – as I argued in Chapter 5 – it is quantity that matters most. It's less applicable to other stages of writing, such as redrafting, where quality is more important.

Whichever method you use, it needs to harmonise with your natural rhythms – with your writing metabolism, as it were. If, for example, you are by nature a sprinter, happiest when writing in short bursts, it will be better to plan half-hour slots than two-hour ones. The usual mistake is to be over-ambitious: to strive to write for longer periods than you can sustain. That, like an over-ambitious diet, will end in failure and demoralisation. It is better to start by writing a little and often, and then either to keep it that way (twenty sessions of writing, each of say fifteen minutes, will generate a surprisingly large amount of text) or gradually to make small increments of, for example, five minutes or 100 words of text.

I recommend slightly exceeding your limit – by writing, say, 50 words more than you budgeted, or writing for an extra minute or two. The most important point, however, is to aim to finish on a high. This is not what most authors do. The natural thing to do is to keep writing whilst it's going well and then stop when the going gets harder. The problem with that is it discourages you from returning – who wants to go back to something difficult or return to a negative experience? Stopping whilst the writing is progressing successfully makes the prospect of return more inviting.

Each time you succeed in keeping to your schedule by starting and finishing at the appointed times, give yourself some kind of reward, however small. Draw a smiley on your schedule, share the good news with someone else, treat yourself to a latte. Rewards reinforce the habit. Whenever you reach a larger milestone – the end of an entire chapter, for example – allow yourself a larger reward. Go out for a pizza or whatever. And if, each time you do this, you take someone – your partner, say – with you, they will start to have a vested interest in helping you to reach your targets.

As well as planning on a weekly basis, it is important to plan using longer time scales. It can usually be discerned in advance that different seasons support different schedules. I lost count long ago of authors who have told me that they have got behind schedule 'because of exam marking'. Perhaps they wonder why I am unsympathetic – have I no idea how long exam marking takes? Well, yes, I have; and I also know that it comes around at the same time each year, is utterly predictable, and can therefore be taken account of in the schedule.

When planning over longer time scales, avoid the temptation to fall into an all-or-nothing mindset. Consider, for example, the beginning of the academic year. It may well be true to say that for a few weeks you'll be able to do less writing than usual and so need to edit your schedule. It will not be true to say that you 'can't do *any* writing that month'.

The opposite, equally seductive, temptation is to look ahead to golden times when you 'won't have much to do' other than write. 'My classes will be over by then': good, but will your administrative duties? When I was an inexperienced editor I always used to welcome the news that one of my authors had a sabbatical or period of study leave coming up. I would believe them when they told me they'd 'be able to write the book then'. As a matter of record, authors rarely write as much as they expect to in such periods. If I had a choice between working with an author who had a sabbatical approaching or one who had developed the habit of writing little and often, I'd choose the latter every time.

One final point about long-range planning when you are devising a schedule for a book: the natural thing is to decide the optimum rate of working by dividing the total time available by the number of chapters. If, for example, you have twelve months in which to write a book comprising eight chapters, that works out at an average of one and a half months (i.e. about forty-five days) per chapter. This way of thinking allows no time either for what we might call the 'other bits' – the prelim pages, such as the preface and acknowledgements, or end matter, such as appendices. Neither does it allow time for collating and formatting the typescript as a whole at the end of the process. Such tasks take time – usually more than one thinks. As a solution, therefore, I recommend that when dividing the time available by the number of chapters, you add a notional chapter and a half. If, as in the above example, your book consists of eight chapters, then, for the purposes of calculating time, treat it as 9.5 chapters. The difference in the time to be allocated to each chapter will be significant (here, about thirty-eight days, rather than forty-five).

SUMMARY

1. When designing a schedule, begin by blocking out times that you know you will not be able to devote to your writing.
2. Identify A-time.
3. Identify B-time.
4. Write regularly – try to avoid more than one blank day in a row.
5. Establish a routine: as often as possible, try to write at the same time of day.
6. Beware over-ambitious schedules. They are self-defeating.
7. Stop writing whilst the writing session is still going well.
8. Reward yourself for your successes.
9. Think long-term as well as short-.

CHAPTER 10

People

Writing a book inevitably involves working with other people. They may be divided, at least in a rough and ready way, into three main groups: Group (a) those whose prime function is to help create content, (b) those whose prime function is to process text, and (c) those who work on the book beyond the text. (a) includes co-authors, contributors, and volume editors; (b) includes peer-reviewers, various kinds of editors, and proofreaders; and (c) includes designers and marketing staff.

CONTENT ORIGINATORS

Let's consider the originators first. It may be that you are considering writing the book with a co-author. The potential advantages to be gained from such an arrangement are not limited to the obvious point that the workload may be shared. The arrangement also allows authors to specialise, each writing the parts of the book they are best suited to. Co-authorship may also provide a built-in form of project management and quality control as the writers monitor, and provide feedback on, each other's drafts. And, when it comes to publication, there will be two authors, each with a stake in promoting the book.

However, co-authorship can also lead to problems. The pressure to explain, discuss, and respond to each other's writing can be unwelcome. Problems can arise as it becomes clear, as the project progresses, that the authors have in fact different visions of the book. Diverse styles of writing can be difficult to mesh. Sensitivities are easily aroused: writing is a personal business and comments on style may all too easily become, or be interpreted as, comments on personality.

The good news is that there are measures one can take to reduce the likelihood of difficulties arising. First, it helps to discuss the project in detail. In particular, it is best to make the process of creating a book proposal a genuinely collaborative, interactive, process.

Second, consider not only the book itself but also the project management involved. Discuss each other's workstyles. Explore potential areas of tension in advance. Be explicit about who is going to do what, when, and also what each party is *not* going to do. Discuss status. Are you equal partners or will one of you be the lead author? Who should the publisher communicate with? Whose name will come first on the copyright notice and the title page?

Be sure to record the agreement between you in writing. This may sound unduly formal. However, over a number of months it's very easy for memories of exactly what was agreed to begin to diverge. A written record minimises this risk.

It is likely that, as the project takes shape and ideas and circumstances change, you will not want to be bound by exactly what was agreed at the outset: yet the danger is that the agreement then begins to unravel. It is useful, therefore, to agree a procedure for amending the agreement – and for recording changes in writing. Again, this might seem over-formal – but if it prevents disputes arising, that is a price worth paying.

Third, each co-author should produce some actual text as early in the process as possible. Often it's only at this point that differences of opinion become clear. For example, one author might favour a scholarly style, the other a more journalistic one. Or one author might often write in the first person whilst the other never does. So long as one merely talks *about* the book, as in a proposal, differences over assumptions such as these may remain hidden; writing sample text smokes them out.

Sometimes a project involves three co-authors. Often, in such cases, they are not, and not intended to be, all equal parties. It is common in such circumstances for one of the three to play a specialist role, perhaps contributing just one or two chapters. Such arrangements often work well, extending the advantages that accrue from division of labour without unduly complicating the project management.

Having three co-authors involved as more or less equal partners can also work well. The unequal number helps to avoid positions of stalemate. It can, however, make communication unwieldy: authorship can begin to resemble committee work – and that rarely produces good writing.

As a commissioning editor I feel well disposed towards projects proposed by pairs of co-authors, but more ambivalent towards trios. I'm even more sceptical of quartets: when four authors are involved, the danger of a committee mentality setting in is even greater – each decision gets referred and deferred and when, eventually, they get made, there always seems to be someone who is unhappy with the outcome. That said, I took delivery of a typescript a month ago written by a team of five authors from three universities: it was delivered on schedule and to specification, written in a consistent style and to a high standard. In that case, however, there was, by agreement, a strong lead author who acted almost like a volume editor.

Rather than co-authoring a book, it may be you are considering editing a collection. Such projects may reap some of the advantages of co-authorship – in particular, they allow contributors each to concentrate on their specialisms. Edited volumes often benefit novice authors, helping them to get published in book form for the first time and to learn more about the business of authorship in the process. And some books do need to be edited, if they are to be written at all. This is true of most reference books, because of their scale and scope.

However, if you are considering becoming a volume editor, it is important to go into such a project with your eyes open. Be careful, in particular, not simply to assume that editing will be much less work – or, indeed, any less work at all – than writing a book. Edited projects tend to be wedge-shaped. At the outset, the amount of work required from the volume editor looks small. You decide what the book is about and who the contributors will be; you agree word limits and delivery dates with them; you send them the publishers' style guide; and, then, when the chapters are delivered, you collate them into a single document, do a little topping and tailing, and, as a finishing touch, compose an elegant introduction.

Perhaps it does sometimes work like that, although I don't remember ever having encountered such a project. What might happen instead is as follows. You do indeed decide what the book will be about and who will be in it, though getting a commitment from some contributors – and a paragraph from each to include in the book proposal – may prove harder work than expected. And you do indeed agree extents and delivery dates, though some contributors may murmur that they 'will need more space' because their 'chapter is different', and some will say that they will try to meet the deadline though they 'have a lot on'. Some others might need a good nudge before they respond to your e-mails at all.

By the time of the deadline for contributors to deliver their chapters to you, you have only two chapters – one of them written by yourself. You send reminders. Some of the contributors actually reply: 'I've nearly finished'; 'I'm working on this but will need another couple of months'; 'I haven't made any progress on this [i.e. done anything at all]; when do you need it by?'; 'Could you ask Mike if he'd like to do this one, since I'm snowed under at the moment?'; 'I didn't realise this was still on: because I hadn't heard from you I'd assumed it wasn't going ahead'; and 'Sorry, I won't be able to do it after all.'

This process goes through several iterations, the divergence between contributors' performance growing all the while. As contributions do gradually arrive, you begin to see that they are not always what was hoped for. Though the style guide was crystal clear, contributors have used a variety of referencing styles. One hasn't provided any references at all ('I didn't realise you needed them yet'). One contribution simply tails off half-way through the chapter, another – this time apparently complete – turns out on closer inspection to contain a number of ellipses ('case study to follow'). Another comes attached to an e-mail that says 'you only wanted a draft at this stage, right?'

Overall, the quality is mixed but disappointing. One of the chapters is frankly poor. Another one bears little relation to the original specification and looks suspiciously like either a conference paper or a rejected journal article plucked from the contributor's bottom drawer.

Much negotiation and renegotiation follows. The publisher is concerned: the project is late, its specifications have changed, and the star contributor has dropped out. And by this time the one contributor who did deliver punctually is becoming agitated because the 'data in the chapter will be out of date by the time this book is published'.

Your efforts to edit the book into consistent style have led you first to question where the line between editing and rewriting might lie and then to step over it: increasingly it seems that the only way the book will ever get finished is for you to write it yourself. The contributor who has dropped out entirely – a colleague who works in the same corridor as you and whom you had (until now) regarded as a friend – was to have written the one chapter that is clearly indispensable to the book. The only solution is to take yourself off to the library, take out three or four books on the topic, and try to write 2–3,000 words that don't say very much and so don't, you pray, contain too many errors. Confidentially, you ask another colleague to look over it 'just to make sure there's nothing glaring'. By now, you have reached the other end of the wedge – and found it is very thick indeed. You remind yourself of the quotation from Jean-Paul Sartre: 'L'enfer, c'est les autres' ('Hell is other people').

When the book is published, some of the contributors seem very pleased with themselves. None of them thanks you. Reviewers comment that the treatment is less than coherent and the quality uneven. Your publisher mentions that the book 'isn't selling'.

The above account is, of course, a caricature – and one that is, no doubt, unfair to you, since you would not stoop to the levels described above. It isn't, however, very much of a caricature. Though the circumstances I have narrated do not usually, thank goodness, all coalesce in one project, none of them is unheard of or even particularly unusual. And sometimes it is worse: sometimes the book does not materialise at all.

Fortunately, there are several measures you can take to minimise the risk of problems arising. The following is a list derived mainly from observation of good practice amongst successful volume editors.

1. Use the book proposal as a test run. Require something specific from each contributor by a certain date. Treat as a hazard light any failure to do what is required when it is required.
2. Give yourself some wiggle room: negotiate with the publisher some flexibility in terms of number of chapters and extent, without feeling obliged to publicise the fact to contributors.
3. Agree with each contributor a precise chapter specification, including an exact title, word limit, and delivery dates for a first

draft and a final draft. Allow yourself enough time between the two dates to read and respond to first drafts.

4. Set a brisk schedule. A chapter usually does not take a great deal of time to write. The problem is getting the chapter to the top of each contributor's to-do list. If you allow six months, most contributors will do little or nothing for the first four months: if you allow twelve, most will merely postpone the task for ten.

5. Give contributors deadlines that are earlier than are strictly necessary. Do not let on.

6. If, when agreeing delivery dates, anyone sucks their teeth or says something like 'I'll do my best, but I've got a lot on', consider dropping them there and then.

7. Get the commissioning editor onside and take him or her into your confidence. Ensure the publishers send out contributor contracts promptly – and chases contributors to return signed copies. If you have worries about particular contributors, alert the editor.

8. Maintain regular contact with contributors, even if you have to find excuses for doing so. Don't rely on e-mail alone. Sometimes hard copy sent through the post will carry more weight. Phone calls are usually more effective for finding out what is going on and for expressing tone (urgency, for example).

9. Use collective communications only for factual information and for sharing good news. Deal with worries or concerns on a strictly individual basis.

10. Set a series of intermediate deadlines. For example, specify that a list of sub-headings for each chapter will be required one month into the project. This provides you with early warning signs regarding procrastination. It also helps the contributors by ensuring that they begin to focus on the project and visualise their contributions. And it helps you to check that the chapters will be on the right lines in terms of structure and content.

11. No less than one month before each deadline, send a reminder.

12. Take care neither to indulge contributors nor to do their work for them. If, for example, the style guide asks for text to be presented double-spaced in 12 point Times New Roman, it is reasonable to expect and even insist that contributors do so. It takes each contributor very little time to do this, whereas, if you end

up having to reformat, say, a dozen chapters, it will take a good deal of your time.

13. Whenever a problem arises, or seems to be arising, act on it. If you don't – if you just hope it will sort itself out or won't recur – you will probably be storing up problems for yourself later. Nip problems in the bud.

14. Always, always, have at least a Plan B.

Are such measures really necessary? In my experience, yes. Isn't this all a little over the top? And aren't I being unduly cynical? In my experience, no.

By now you may be wondering whether it is advisable ever to become a volume editor. On a personal level, I confess that, if the United Nations passed a resolution banning all edited books bar genuine reference works, I don't think the world would be a worse place as a result. I must, though, balance my own view with that of practitioners. Many academics who have edited books have described the experience as a 'learning process'. They perhaps choose that cliché because it is ambiguous. In part, it is used as a euphemism (meaning the task was more demanding than expected) – but in part it is meant genuinely: early career academics in particular sometimes find that the experience teaches them a good deal about authorship, publishing, project management, and academia. These are all good reasons for taking on such a project – at least if one also anticipates the potential difficulties.

TEXT PROCESSORS

The second group of people you will work with comprise those we have termed 'text processors'. These include: commissioning editor; peer reviewers; development editors; copy-editors; typesetters; proofreaders; and indexers. The following account follows the traditional, linear, model of publishing.

The commissioning editor

First, you will work with a commissioning editor. This is the person you will have approached, or who will first have approached you, to discuss the idea for your book in the first place. This editor is also the person who will have proposed your book for publication and gained authorisation to offer you a contract. Though the organisation of editorial roles varies between publishing houses, in most companies the commissioning editor will continue to have oversight of the book and sponsor, or 'champion', the project. Commissioning editors therefore play a pivotal role. They are likely to be the main port of call for authors and to be regarded by the publishers as the staff most responsible for ensuring that typescripts are delivered and are of sufficient quality.

The commissioning editor may fulfil such functions in person or delegate some of the work to other people – most notably peer reviewers and development editors. The use of peer reviewers varies between publishers and between projects. They may be consulted at pre-contract stage (where they will be asked to read a proposal or sample chapter) or when the typescript is complete – or at both stages, or not at all. Textbooks are likely to be heavily reviewed by lecturers because publishers want to ensure that the book is suitable for adoption. The larger the revenue forecast for a textbook, the more the publisher will want to use reviewers as a means of limiting the risk of the project failing – and the larger the budget is likely to be for remunerating reviewers. With monographs, reviewers may be used, in effect, to protect a brand's reputation for academic quality. Because the profit margin on a single monograph is likely to be modest, however, the provision for reviewing is likely to be more meagre.

Peer reviewers

How should you respond when you receive reviewers' comments? First, identify the positive comments, commending aspects of your work. Allow yourself a pat on the back for each of these – but don't only do that. Also seek to build on the positive aspects. If a reviewer of your proposal, for example, says that they 'particularly like' some feature or that it will 'particularly appeal to the market', run with it: consider how you can revise the project to make more of whatever strength the reviewer has responded to – and let your commissioning editor know.

Now consider the reviewers' critical comments and divide them into two categories. First, identify those that you agree with. Ask yourself: is this important enough to require action? If so, what action is required? And are you able, and willing, to take the necessary action: do you have the expertise and resources?

Second, identify those criticisms you disagree with. It is tempting to disagree with all the critical comments. This is natural, but should be resisted. After all, the publishers are in effect providing you with a free consultancy service, so it would be a shame not to take the opportunity to learn from the experience. It usually helps to allow some time to elapse between reading the reviews and responding to them. This helps to take the heat out of the process.

Now divide those criticisms you disagree with into two further categories: (a) those where, though you think the reviewer is mistaken, you can see why the reviewer has made the criticism in question; and (b) those where you believe the reviewer is just wrong. The key to responding intelligently to reviews usually lies in accurately identifying type (a) comments. These are what I call 'symptomatic misreadings': the reviewer has misunderstood your work, but that is because you have not been careful enough to preclude such misunderstanding. Remember here the sheepdog analogy developed in Chapter 6 (pp. 77–80): it is the job of the sheepdog (author) to anticipate how sheep (readers) might stray, and thus to prevent them from doing so. If the reviewer has got the wrong end of the stick, so might other readers – unless you revise your text before it is published.

With those criticisms you believe to be plain wrong, do not simply dismiss them: explain fully and courteously why you believe them to be mistaken. Consider whether some version of this apologia should actually be included in the text of the work itself.

In effect, you will have worked through the decision tree illustrated in Figure 10.1. As a result, the responses you send back to the editor will fall under the following headings:

1. reviewers' positive comments;
2. reviewers' criticisms that you agree with;
3. reviewers' comments you disagree with: (a) those you see as symptomatic misreading, and (b) those you believe simply to be wide of the mark.

In each case, make it clear whether you propose to redraft your work and explain, if so, in what way, and, if not, why not. The more

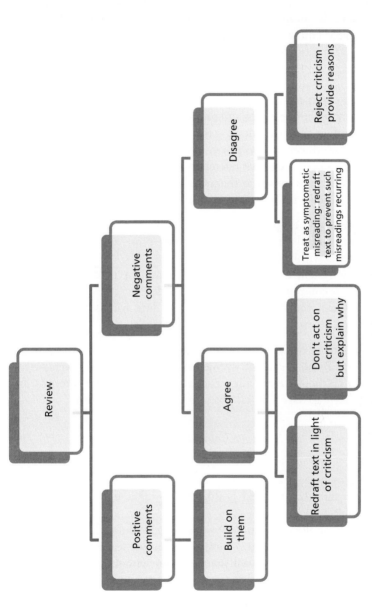

Fig. 10.1 Decision tree for responding to peer reviews

scrupulous you are about identifying comments of types (2) and (3a), and the more constructive your responses to them are, the more likely your editor is to respect your views about (3b).

The development editor

The development editor in effect forms a link in the chain between the commissioning editor and the copy-editor. If commissioning editors work at the macro-level – the overall conception of the book – and copy-editors at the micro-level (correcting the grammar, for example, or checking that references are complete), the development editor will work mostly at the meso-level. A development editor will be concerned with questions such as:

- How should chapters be grouped into parts of the book?
- What should be the balance between prose and other kinds of material within each chapter?
- What system of cross-referencing should be used? How should various components of a work be labelled?
- How can the work be brought into line with series style and requirements?

Development editing, then, is very much a craft, concerned with shaping texts. By no means every project will be allocated to a development editor. Textbooks, especially those carrying high revenue forecasts, are most likely to have a development editor allocated to them.

Copy-editors

Copy-editors work with text on a micro-level. They read through texts closely, page by page and sentence by sentence. Their function is to ensure that the text is ship-shape – that it is clear, accurate, complete, and correct.

Much of the copy-editor's work may be done through directly intervening with the text – correcting grammatical errors, for example. Some of it, however, will involve liaison with the author. Typically the copy-editor will send the author a list of queries. For example:

'Is the "John Smith" mentioned on p. 139 the same person as the "Smith" on p. 82?'

'On p. 38 you give one date for this event and on p. 72 a different one: which is correct?'

'What is the source of the quotation on p. 108?'

'Please supply Table 3.6, which is missing.'

Good copy-editors always gain my grudging admiration. Grudging, because often the detailed work of copy-editing, by its very nature, appears pedantic; admiration, because copy-editors pick up problems that have passed everyone else by. When I wrote my first book, I set out to provide such a clean typescript that the copy-editor would have nothing to do – but nevertheless I received two or three pages of queries. Howard Becker (in *Writing for Social Scientists*) has likened the effect on a text of proficient copy-editing to the effect of adjusting the focus of a camera: suddenly everything becomes sharp and clear.

Find out from the publisher when you may expect to receive copy-editing queries and block off some time in your schedule to deal with them. If there are a lot of queries, resist the temptation to feel dismayed. The more carefully the text has been edited, the more queries there are likely to be. Each query raised at this stage provides an opportunity to remove a potential cause of dissatisfaction amongst your readers at a later date. Queries should, therefore, be dealt with promptly, attentively, and courteously.

Typesetters

The main function of typesetters is to change the physical form of the typescript from that in which the author has provided it to that in which the printer receives it and, ultimately, the reader sees it. Typically this involves laying out the text according to a predetermined text design and, in the process, converting a file from a word-processing document into some other format, such as PDF or XML. Usually the work of typesetting is outsourced by the publisher and there is little, if any, direct contact between the author and the typesetter.

Occasionally the work of the typesetter is, in effect, outsourced to the authors. That is, authors may be provided with a design specification (usually known as a shell) within which to write text from the outset. This occurs most often with monographs, where the reason is a desire to save typesetting costs. Developments in software make it more likely in future that authors will be required to typeset their own work.

Proofreaders

Once the text has been typeset, it needs to be proofread. With many projects, proofs are sent both to the author and to a professional proofreader, who will each read and check proofs independently. In the case of low-budget projects, however, the author might be the only proofreader. If you are not sure what the arrangement is for your book, do find out.

It is desirable to have the proofs read by a professional as well as by yourself. Proofreading is a skill in its own right and not all authors are good at it. In any case, another pair of eyes is always likely to be a good thing. That said, you should always proofread your work *as if* you were the only person doing so. In proofreading, thoroughness is all.

Much time will have elapsed between submitting the typescript to the publisher and receiving proofs to read. And, in the process, the look of the text will have changed through being typeset. Both points will help you to see the text with a fresh pair of eyes.

Avoid trying to proofread on the hoof. Proofreading requires calm and focused attention. Choose a suitable location and block off periods of time that are long enough to allow you to get properly into the task but not so long that you tire and become careless. For most people, periods of between one and two hours work best. To help you manage your time, ask the editor as early as possible to send you a publishing schedule indicating when you should expect to receive proofs and when they need to be returned by.

When you are proofreading, give special attention to notes, references, and cross-references. Check that they are complete and accurate. Also look carefully at the headings and check that each has been given the right weight (that main headings are distinct from sub-headings, that sub-headings are distinguished from sub-sub-headings, and so on, throughout the hierarchy of headings).

The function of proofreading is to check for errors in the text as it stands, not to rewrite the text. When reading the text, you may well spot passages that could have been better written. And you may well think of points you wish you had added. If so, resist any temptation to redraft the text at this stage. Such attempts are likely, in any case, to be blocked (entirely reasonably) by the publisher; in the unlikely event of such revisions being included, they will cause delays and are likely, because you are bucking the system, to introduce new errors. Changes of this kind will also incur costs (especially if the pagination changes as a result): these, according to standard publishing contracts, will be charged to the author. Attempting to redraft the text at this stage will also identify you as an author whom the publisher should avoid working with ever again. In short: stick to making corrections, don't try to redraft!

Because proofreading is a skill in its own right, you might wish to consider taking a course. Professional organisations, such as the Society for Editors and Proofreaders, provide a number of such courses, some requiring attendance in person and others requiring participation online. The level, duration, and cost of courses vary, but a one-day course should be enough to cover the basics and shouldn't be expensive. The work of academics frequently involves producing or processing documents – memos, reports, teaching materials, and so on – so the benefits of being proficient in this skill extend beyond its application to one's book.

Indexers

Most publishing contracts state that indexing will be done either by the author or by an indexer and that, if it is done by the latter, the costs will be charged to the author (usually through deduction from royalties). Authors frequently ask me which option I recommend. In fact, either option carries with it both advantages and disadvantages. Compiling the index yourself enables you to save the cost of the indexer's fees. It also provides an opportunity to ensure that the index reflects the conceptual framework of the book. On the other hand, indexing requires both skill and time – and indexers' fees are usually modest.

It is important to recognise what indexing is. From the fact that most indexes are arranged alphabetically, it certainly does not follow that the essence of indexing lies in arranging items into alphabetical order. An index is very different from a concordance. The essence of indexing lies in taxonomy. That is, an index is a means of indicating not only the scope of the work but also how a text is organised and how items within the text are related to each other. For that reason, the compilation of an index requires a number of judgements to be made. The indexer needs to make a decision about what is known in the trade as specificity. A text may contain items at a number of levels of significance (think of them as 'main', 'sub-', 'sub-sub-', 'sub-sub-sub-', and so on). How far down the hierarchy of items should the index go (that is, how *specific* should the index be?)? The indexer also needs to make a decision about the degree of exhaustivity. At each level of the hierarchy, how many items should the index include? Though it is tempting to say, 'All of them', inclusion of trivial items can make indexes unwieldy without adding anything to the reader's comprehension.

Readers' needs are, of course, paramount: it is for the sake of readers that the index is being provided. Indexing therefore requires empathy – it requires an understanding of how potential readers are likely to think and what they will want to use the index for. One of the advantages of using a third party to compile the index for your book is that the indexer will themselves be a reader and therefore more likely to start from the reader's point of view than the writer's.

Over the years my default position has changed from recommending that authors do their own indexes to recommending that they outsource the work to professional indexers. One reason for my change of heart is the recognition that indexes produced by authors often turn out not to be very good. The main reason, however, is the argument that I heard put by Dr Martina Leonarz, an author from the University of Zurich. She explained that she would routinely prefer to pay for an indexer – in part because she thought that an indexer, as a specialist, would do the job better, but mainly because such an arrangement would leave her free to spend the time on the activities she was best at, namely research and writing. That sounded like good (business) sense to me.

I should add a recommendation here. When you are negotiating your publishing contract, ensure that it stipulates that any indexer selected to work on your book is professionally competent, qualified, and a member of the main professional body in your country – for example, in America, the American Society for Indexing; in Canada, the Indexing Society of Canada; and, in the UK, the Society of Indexers. No publisher should have difficulty in agreeing to such a stipulation.

In the previous sections of this chapter we have examined the work of 'content originators' and 'text processors'. In this final section, we concentrate on those whose work takes us beyond the text and who consider the book as an artefact and product. We will focus on collaboration with designers and marketing staff.

Designers

Your book will incorporate two types of design. First, there is the internal design, involving decisions over page layout, font, line-spacing, and so on. Second, there is the cover design.

If you are concerned about the internal design, it is important to raise this with the editor as early in the process as possible – certainly before you have delivered the typescript. One should recognise, however, that any influence you have is likely to be limited. Changes to designs incur costs. And your publishers are likely to regard text design as an aspect of their brand. If you feel that the proposed design would create problems for readers, you should certainly pursue the matter. But make your comments as objective as possible. The more they are anchored in a genuine concern for readers, rather than merely your own aesthetic preferences, the more likely they are to carry weight.

Most authors like to be consulted over cover designs. Standard contracts often do not guarantee this, so you should seek to ensure, when you negotiate your contract, that such a guarantee is included. In particular, ask for it to apply to both the visual design and any text to be used on the cover. Ask too for it to extend to the whole cover, not just the front.

As an editor, I understand authors' wishes to be consulted and believe it is wise of publishers to accede to this request. That said, such consultations sometimes generate more heat and less light than they should. Let me give a couple of examples of the kinds of problem that arise.

The first example is an extreme one. An author phoned me in response to a draft cover that we had sent her. She told me that the blurb was completely unacceptable. When I asked her why, she said it 'misrepresented her life's work'. When I asked the source of the difficulty, it turned out to be one word that she was unhappy with. She clearly felt strongly: she used emotive language, burst into tears, and rang off. By the time we resumed the conversation, I had been able to check the facts. I told her that I was surprised to hear that she thought the blurb misrepresented her work and that I was not inclined to alter it. When she asked me why, I explained it was because the e-mail trail revealed very clearly that the blurb had been written by the author herself.

We all make mistakes, of course. I too have, on occasion, failed to recognise text that I originated. The problem here, though, is not so much the mistake – it was the role that the author adopted. In her book (pun intended, I admit), we certainly weren't partners working together on a project: rather, she was the prima donna and I was the audience. In my experience, adopting the prima donna role in publishing is self-defeating.

The second example concerns an author who contacted me after her book had been published by a company I had once worked for. She wanted to know whether I could intervene on her behalf. Though I was certain I couldn't, I asked her what the problem was. She was unhappy with her cover, on the grounds that: (a) the image was ideologically inappropriate for one of its intended markets; (b) the image gave a misleading impression about the stance taken by the author in the text itself; and (c) the cover was aesthetically unappealing. I did get an opportunity to look at the book. In my own view, the author was right about (a) – though I felt she had overstated the consequences. I felt there was some truth too in her argument about (b), though again I felt she was overstating the problem. On (c) I disagreed: the cover seemed to me reasonably attractive. The point here, however, is not the extent to which the author was right or wrong. It is that the publishers, inadvertently I think, had not consulted her over the cover. Had they done so, there might have been an opportunity to change the cover, the author's perception of it, or both. Once the book had been printed, there was no opportunity to do either.

Of the two examples above, the first is an extreme case. The second is an example of the kind of thing that does happen every now and then, albeit inadvertently. Here then are some suggestions designed to minimise the potential for problems to arise.

First, when you are negotiating the contract, seek to ensure that there is a guarantee that your name will be given due prominence on the cover of the book. (Though 'due prominence' is a poorly defined phrase, it isn't entirely meaningless.) But do not simply rely on contractual obligations – the publishers may simply forget about them. Try to discover the schedule for cover design and, in due course, send a timely reminder to your editor.

Also discuss with your editor as early in the process as possible what the publishers' thinking is with regard to the cover. Seek to establish, for example, whether the cover will have a series design and whether or not the budget is intended to cover the use of a photograph or illustration.

When you are sent a draft cover, check first whether there are any errors. Errors may be either verbal or visual. For example, an image used on the cover of a history book may be anachronistic. As well as actual errors, check too for any inappropriateness. For example, some images are ideologically inappropriate in certain markets. Such judgements usually require more discussion than straightforward factual or technical errors.

If I had to give just one tip on responding to cover designs, it would be to look carefully at the design of the spine. The spine is often overlooked, yet it is important: in bookshops, most books are displayed side-on rather than face-out. Ensure that the font on the spine is large and clear and that the design is uncluttered.

Feel free to express your aesthetic preferences regarding cover design, but recognise at the same time that such preferences do not represent incontrovertible judgements. Remember, too, that there will be commercial constraints on cover design – in particular, questions of cost and of the publishers' branding. There is also the question of the appropriateness of the cover design for the market the book is aimed at. The most appropriate cover will not necessarily be the most artistic or tasteful. As an editor I have on some occasions rejected cover designs on the grounds that they have been too tasteful: I've asked the designer to come up with something more brash. Whether the authors would always have shared my views, I am not sure – but I am confident that such interventions helped to make the books in question more saleable.

Overall, it is important to recognise that the right to be consulted is not the same as the right of approval. Authors' views should certainly be listened to – the consultation is not genuine if they aren't – but that is not to say that they should necessarily be assented to. Similarly, a right to be consulted is not to be equated with the right to design the cover oneself. On some occasions, when authors have overstepped this mark and sought to insist on the use of some particular image or style, I have had to remind them that authors are not necessarily any better at designing books than designers would be at writing them!

The marketing department

Except in special circumstances, the main responsibility for marketing a book is the publishers'. That said, they will certainly request some assistance from the author. Marketing will be most productive if it is viewed by both parties as a collaborative activity.

Before we look at the detail of that collaboration, let us get clear what exactly marketing is – and also what it is not. Authors sometimes equate marketing with either advertising or publicity. Advertising and publicity may indeed be useful as means of marketing (though not invariably so), but it is important to distinguish between these processes.

The marketing of academic books is best understood as a three-step process. First, the market needs to be understood. This involves asking such questions: as 'What is the market for this book?' 'What kind of customers does it consist of?' 'Where is the market to be found?' 'What is the relationship between the book in question and other products in the same market?'

As a second step, one needs to ensure that the product fits the market. No amount of marketing will sell a book if it isn't suitable. This involves deciding what will and won't work in the market and ensuring that the book is written, designed, packaged, and sold accordingly.

The third step consists of ensuring that the market knows about and understands the product. It also involves getting the product into the market place. There are a variety of means available for informing the market, including advertising and publicity. The appropriate means will vary according to the type of book.

Authors can make valuable contributions to all three steps. The first step begins with the book proposal. As we have seen, detailed, accurate information in the book proposal is invaluable. When the book has been commissioned, the author will usually be asked to supplement this information by completing an author questionnaire (AQ). This will cover such questions as which periodicals might review the book, which conferences might provide marketing opportunities, and who might be willing to provide endorsements for the book. As with the book proposal, it is certainly worth providing accurate, detailed information. The more you make things easy for marketing staff, the more likely they are to make use of the information. It certainly does not follow, however, that all of the information that you provide will be acted upon. Bear in mind that the AQ is a standard, one-size-fits-all, pro forma. Just because there is a question asking for, say, suggestions of suitable occasions for a book launch, it doesn't necessarily follow that your book will be given a launch event.

Be sure to include details of marketing opportunities local to where you live or work. It is usually much easier to win the attention of local media than state or national media. If your book is covered by the local media, this may be useful in itself. Moreover, local media content is monitored by national media, and so such coverage can lead by the back door to coverage on a wider stage.

The second step of the marketing process – i.e. ensuring that the product is suited to the market – is in many ways the publishers' responsibility. They need to make appropriate decisions about such matters as format, price, cover design, and publication date. However, the author also has an important responsibility at this stage. This consists in the main of ensuring that the book is written according to the specification agreed when the book was contracted. If it's supposed to be 80,000 words, make sure that it isn't 60,000 or 100,000; if you said that you would obtain a foreword from a prominent professor, be sure to do so; if you agreed to write the book at an introductory level, then resist the temptation to make the treatment more sophisticated, and so on. Stick to the brief.

The third step in the marketing process – i.e. getting the book, and information about it, into the market place – is again primarily the responsibility of the publishers. However, success is more likely if the publishers and the author work in collaboration. Much of the most important activity occurs behind the scenes. It consists of 'B2B' ('business to business') marketing to intermediaries such as wholesalers, retailers, library suppliers, and export agents. Many of the processes involved are dull but essential. They include, for example, obtaining an ISBN for each publication and ensuring that this, together with other bibliographical detail (e.g. format and price), is provided in accurate and timely fashion to the book industry through electronic databases.

What treatment a book receives beyond B2B marketing will depend on what genre it belongs to. For reference publishing, the institutional (i.e. library) market will be important. In this market, the provision of full, accurate information is particularly important: librarians are information professionals and expect to know precisely what it is they are acquiring when they purchase a product. The development of reference products is often capital-intensive and so publishers are keen to obtain 'day 1' sales, i.e. sales on publication. Much of the marketing, therefore, is likely to be done well ahead of publication, often supported by discounts on pre-publication orders. Because reference products are expensive, the publishers' brand is important: it needs to establish a reputation for quality. The role of the author in marketing to the institutional market is very limited. Authors can contribute, however, by recommending that their own libraries buy their works and by encouraging colleagues in other institutions to make recommendations to their libraries.

The marketing of monographs is in many ways similar to the marketing of reference products because much of the market, especially for hardback editions, consists of library purchases. However, there is often an opportunity to make some sales to individuals too. For example, publishers may offer a hardback monograph for sale at a discounted rate from bookstands at academic conferences. A paperback edition will have greater potential for sales, either direct (through conferences, say) or via Internet retailers. However, many bricks-and-mortar bookshops, even on campuses, will be reluctant to stock a monograph, though they will obtain copies for customers who wish to order them.

As with reference publishing, the role of the monograph author in this step of the marketing is usually limited. It does no harm, however, to display some marketing savvy. Adding details of the book to one's e-mail signature and webpage, for example, will help to get it known, as will ensuring that complimentary copies get into the hands of influential people in the relevant field.

The main process for marketing adoptables is providing plentiful, accurate information to potential adopters – i.e. course lecturers (plus the libraries that support them) – in good time. Genuine potential adopters also need to be able to obtain inspection copies without difficulty. Lecturers need time to consider books and decide whether to change course reading. For courses starting at the beginning of autumn, the marketing needs to be done in the first quarter of the calendar year. Again, the role of authors at this stage is limited: it consists in the main of using one's savvy to help ensure that lecturers in your field get to hear of the book. Do not be shy about using your networks – for example, by asking your subject association to mention the book in their newsletter or offering to write a short article about the book.

The marketing of books designed to cross over into the consumer market will be very different. Much will depend on the publishers' management of key accounts. In particular, they will need to gain the attention of retail chains' central buyers prior to publication. Publishers and retailers will have needed to agree a discount and returns policy that works for both parties.

For cross-over books, publicity may be very important. The managing director of one consumer publisher said to me, 'We don't have a marketing department: we have a *publicity* department' (he was exaggerating, but not much). Media appearances, e-newsletters and RSS feeds, speaking engagements, viral marketing, word-of-mouth recommendation – all are important ingredients.

There may even be a role for advertising direct to the consumer. However, I once heard the editor of a major newspaper discuss his decision to publish a books supplement in the newspaper's weekend edition. He went to an advertising sales company to discuss how to increase the advertising revenue from publishers. Evidently the sales company were not encouraging: 'they laughed'.

There is, I think, a good reason for scepticism over advertising: in publishing, especially academic publishing, advertising is often a waste of scarce marketing resources. I once turned down a very thoughtful, well-written, book on green politics by an eminent author. The competitor that signed up the book placed numerous advertisements on the subway. When I looked up the retail sales figures, they were much as I had forecast: the advertising had not grown the sales but had no doubt eroded the profit margin. Authors often try to chivvy publishers into advertising their books. I suspect that, on the rare occasions they do so successfully, the result is usually an inefficient use of a finite marketing budget. Often, there is more of a case for a kind of advertising that authors usually do not see, namely advertising in B2B publications such as wholesalers' catalogues and the industry press.

Though advertising may have only a modest role, the other forms of publicity we have mentioned may well be productive – and here there is certainly a role for the author. Being available to be interviewed on the radio or filmed for a video on YouTube, to speak at bookshop launches or literary festivals, or to write blogs and articles is important. Many publishing contracts specify that the author must be available for publicity events around the time of publication. It is important to discuss the publication date with the publishers so that you can build such events into your schedule. Bear in mind that publicity, and hence the demand it makes on your time, can snowball: one good interview, for example, may lead to further invitations.

Most higher education institutions now devote considerable resources to media relations. If your institution has a press or public relations office, why not make use of it? Much of the work of such offices is rather humdrum and so staff may find the opportunity to publicise your book refreshing. Be sure to approach them in good time – well before publication. The ideal is to get your press or PR office and your publishers' marketing department to talk to each other.

Overall, then, the role of the author in marketing varies considerably. There is, however, always some role – and the happiest results occur when authors and publishers work in tandem. Often the most important contributions from academic authors come early in the process, in what we have called the first and second steps of marketing. Providing first a book proposal and then an author questionnaire that are both accurate and informative is invaluable: these documents provide the foundation stones for effective marketing plans on the part of the publisher.

SUMMARY

1. Being published is not a solitary activity and should be as collaborative as possible.
2. Authorship involves project management, especially if you are working with other authors.
3. If you are going to edit a volume, go into the process with your eyes open, recognise that the project will be wedge-shaped (i.e. the time commitment will grow), do not assume that editing will be less work than writing a book yourself, and always have at least a Plan B.
4. Differentiate your responses to peer review as much as possible.
5. Schedule time to read proofs properly. Read what is actually there in the proofs, not what you expect to be there.
6. Indexing involves providing a taxonomy for the benefit of the reader. It may be better to leave it to a professional.
7. The right to be consulted over a cover does not equate to a right of veto or the right to design a cover oneself.
8. When responding to cover designs, remember that a book cover is both an aesthetic document and a commercial one. Check in particular that the text on the spine is clear and bold.
9. 'Marketing' is not a synonym for either 'publicity' or 'advertising'. Marketing involves (a) understanding the market; (b) ensuring a good fit between market and product; (c) getting the product, and information about it, into the market.
10. Marketing, and the role of the author in the process, varies between genres.
11. An accurate and informative book proposal and author questionnaire support effective marketing.
12. Recognise the potential of your local media and of your institution's press office.

CHAPTER 11

Next

Two related themes run through this book. The first is the importance of seeing writing as a process – as an activity that happens over time and in which one thing leads to another. The second is the role of anticipation in preventing problems and creating opportunities.

In Chapter 6 (see pp. 74–80) I used the images of the sheepdog and the maze to explore these themes on a micro-level, showing how they impacted on writing in terms of the selection of words and the construction of sentences. In contrast, this chapter is concerned with the bigger picture. The focus shifts from how to write a book, to how to develop an authorial career. The question we explore here is not 'How does one word (or sentence or paragraph) lead to another?' but rather 'How does one work lead to another?'

NEW EDITIONS

The most obvious way in which one publication leads to another is through the publication of a new edition. This is most common with adoptables and reference works (especially annuals). New editions are often popular with publishers: they provide a means of continuing to sell a book over a number of years or even decades. This makes for a better return on investment and also provides a predictable stream of revenue. Authors too are generally pleased to see their books move into new editions, though – as we will see – this can require a good deal of work.

A number of different events may trigger a new edition. For example:

1. the content of the book (e.g. tables of data, references, case studies) might become dated;

2. the approach used in the text might become dated as new perspectives, theories, and research findings emerge or gain in importance;
3. the context in which the book is used might change. For example, the procedures by which students are taught or assessed might alter;
4. a new market might open up, for example in a new export territory;
5. a new, competing, volume might threaten to take market share because it has certain advantages that need to be countered;
6. feedback from users might suggest ways of improving the book.

Over the years, the new edition cycle, at least for adoptables, has been shortening. Where publishers used to think in terms of a new edition every three years or so, now they might publish one every two years. This reflects the increasing pace of change within academia – for example, because of the number of journals in print, new research findings in a field accumulate more quickly than before. The accelerated cycle also reflects a desire to combat the secondhand market. As the market for used books (for example, online and in campus bookstores) has become more organised, so it has tended to erode sales of new copies. Publishers figure that lecturers will adopt the latest edition of a book, with the effect that the market for the previous edition is driven out.

What is a 'new edition'? The term covers a spectrum of possibilities. At one end, the changes involved might be very slight – no more than a new introduction, for example. At the other, a book might be completely overhauled and redesigned. Examples of the changes that might occur between editions include:

- redesign of cover
- redesign of text layout
- change of page size
- correction of errors
- updating of references
- updating of data
- updating of illustrations
- replacement of material, e.g. fresh case studies
- addition of content – new passages or chapters

- redrafting of passages
- incorporation of new approaches or perspectives
- addition or improvement of pedagogical apparatus (questions, exercises, etc.)
- addition or improvement of supporting material (e.g. Powerpoint slides for lecturers)
- condensation or removal of content.

The publishers, drawing on feedback from the market, will usually have firm views on what is required of a new edition. The author is unlikely to lack guidance. One form of feedback used is reviews from lecturers who have adopted the current edition. These need to be supplemented by reviews from potential adopters, i.e. lecturers who have not yet adopted the book, but who might.

I said earlier that new editions can involve the author in a lot of work. How much will depend on the scale of changes. The publishers and the author need to communicate clearly over the question of scale – otherwise misunderstandings may arise. Table 11.1 below is designed to aid communication: it organises the types of changes made in new editions into three levels. This taxonomy is inevitably somewhat rough and ready – the changes required do not always group themselves so neatly – but in practice I find it does help to smoke out differences in understanding between authors and publishers over the scale of changes required.

The aspect of new edition work that is usually done least well is the condensation or omission of extant material. Authors seem happier to add new text than to cut what they have written before. Publishers are often relaxed about this too, reasoning that longer texts can carry higher prices. Yet the result can be books that exceed the ideal length for the market. Students often dislike heavy, bulky books that are difficult to carry; they may feel daunted by the prospect of having to read a large tome; and they resent paying high prices for books that contain large chunks of material that they don't need. I suggest that the first question concerning a new edition should be 'What can come out?'

If you write the kind of book that might go into a second edition, think of the project management involved as a continuous cycle. Even in the few months while the book is in production, your typescript will begin to date. From the moment you deliver the typescript

Table 11.1 *New edition scale*

Level	Typical operations
1. The Light Touch	a) Updating (references, data, perhaps illustrations) b) Redesign of cover c) Correction of errors d) Addition of some passages
2. The Standard Treatment	Level 1 operations plus: a) Replacement of material b) More additional content – possibly new chapters c) Redrafting of passages d) Addition or improvement of pedagogical apparatus e) Addition or improvement of supporting material f) Condensation or removal of content
3. Wholesale	Level 1 & 2 operations plus: a) Redesign of text layout b) Change of page size c) Incorporation of new approaches d) More extensive additional material including new chapters

to the editor, begin to think what is needed for a new edition. You may well have ideas straightaway: perhaps there was an idea that there wasn't time to incorporate into the typescript you have just completed; or there may be a chapter, say, that you weren't entirely happy with. I suggest starting two folders – one made of card and one created on your computer. Use the folders to accumulate ideas and material for use in the next edition. The gradual accumulation of material will reduce the workload when it comes to planning the new edition in earnest.

FURTHER WORKS

The publication of a book can lead to further opportunities in a number of ways. As we discussed at the very beginning of this book (see pp. 5–6), publication might lead to invitations to give talks, write articles, appear in the media, provide consultancy, and so on. This might also lead, directly or indirectly, to further books, especially since it is usually easier for authors to win contracts if they have published before.

Some books lead on to others fairly directly. One might write a sequel; or take a theme or passage from one book and develop it in more detail in the next; or explore the same topic again, though at a different (either more introductory or more advanced) level. On other occasions, the link between books may be more indirect. It may be simply that the publication of one book results in the author beginning to show up on editors' radar so that, as we discussed in chapter 3 (see pp. 28–31), they approach the author with suggestions for further books.

CONCLUSION

In authorship, one thing tends to lead to another. It is rare for a book to sink entirely without trace. For that reason, let us revisit one of the questions that we discussed in the first chapter of this book, namely 'What to write?' (see pp. 8–14). When contemplating whether to develop an idea for a book, bear in mind the image of the (multi-centred, turf) maze that we developed in Chapter 6 (see pp. 74–7). Just as it pays when writing to look ahead and ask what each phrase or sentence may lead to, so it pays to consider what each publication might lead to.

My final piece of advice, therefore, is this: when you find yourself considering a potential publication project, assess not only the project itself, but also what it might lead to.

The title of this book deliberately employs the plural: *Writing Successful Academic Books*. I hope it helps you not only to write a great book and have it published successfully, but also to develop, if you wish, a successful authorial career.

SUMMARY

1. The term 'new edition' can mean any number of things: when discussing a new edition with your publishers, clarify the range and scale of changes envisaged.

2. When working on a new edition, set a premium on condensing or cutting material where possible.
3. Think of new edition development as a continuous cycle: once you have delivered a typescript to your publishers, begin to accumulate material for the next edition.
4. When considering a potential publication, assess not only the project itself, but also what it might lead to.

Appendix A. Proposal guidelines

HOW TO SUBMIT A PERFECT BOOK PROPOSAL

1. Propose a working title
2. Contents:
   a) What genre does the book belong to (e.g. reference / monograph / textbook / student guide / trade book)?
   b) Provide a concise summary of the contents of the book.
   c) Provide a draft contents page. Include not only the chapter headings but also preliminary material, e.g. 'Preface', and end matter, e.g. 'References'.
3. Markets:
   a) What will be the core market? Include quantitative information if available.
   b) What subsidiary markets are there?
   c) Include information about export markets: how will the book appeal to readers abroad? Outline any specific export potential.
4. Competition:
   a) Which are the most closely comparable books (and other resources) available? Please give author, title, publisher, date and place of publication, length, price.
   b) In what way(s) does your book differ?
   c) If there are no competing titles, explain why this is.
5. Sales:
   a) Why will people buy the book? In particular, explain what *needs* the book will fulfil and what *benefits* it will provide to the reader.
   b) Outline any factors relevant to an assessment of the book's potential for sales after its first year.

c) Explain any specific factors regarding the potential for translation rights.

6. Author:
   a) Give your affiliation.
   b) List your relevant qualifications.
   c) List your publications.
   d) What networks do you belong to that might help the publisher to reach the markets you have identified?
   e) Why do you want to write the book? Why does it matter to you?

7. Production data:
   a) How long will the book be in thousands of words all-inclusive (i.e. including preface, notes, references, index, etc.)? Give a 5,000-word range.
   b) What types of figures (e.g. diagrams, photographs) will be required and how many?

8. Date:
   a) When would you deliver the final typescript by? Give either an actual date or number of months from signature of contract.
   b) Identify any important issues concerning the dates of delivery and publication.

9. Anything else?

Appendix B. Sample book proposal

Below is the original proposal for this book. The book itself has departed in some ways from the specification given in the proposal.

Full title

Writing Successful Academic Books: A Complete Guide to Authorship and Publication

Reasons for writing, proposed length, and amount of illustration

Whilst I was Academic Publishing Director at Continuum I often felt frustrated by the amount of repetition involved in academic publishing. New authors make the same mistakes as their predecessors. Editors find themselves saying the same things over and over.

I also learnt from discussion with authors that publishing can seem very mysterious from the outside. Prospective authors are often uncertain about such matters as how to make a pitch or negotiate a contract. Even experienced authors, though less surprised by publishers' decisions, often find the rationale behind those decisions opaque.

There is, therefore, a need for a guide that will explain the twin processes of academic authorship and publication and enable authors to achieve their aims more efficiently. I have found through various talks and workshops that I have given to academics that it is not difficult to provide this guidance. Authors benefit readily from being given an inside view of the publishing industry.

There are of course a number of books already available (I analyse two of the better ones below) but I have never felt entirely happy about recommending any of these. My modest proposal, therefore, is to supply the need by writing the best (most complete, coherent, and accessible) such book.

The book will be 60,000–70,000 words (all-inclusive) with a handful of tables (provided in Word) but no figures.

Intended completion date

I can deliver the complete manuscript within twelve months of contract.

Contents

Prelims

- Foreword (by a publisher or, preferably, successful academic author)
- Acknowledgements
- Preface

1. Foundations

- Reasons for writing
- What to write (the question of genre) and who to write for (audience)
- What makes a book (as opposed to other formats)?

2. Finding a publisher

- Selecting publishers (sources of information; criteria)
- Approaching publishers and getting approached
- Book proposals (purpose and content)
- Publishers' decisions (processes and rationale)
- Contracts (meaning and negotiation)
- Agents (role and benefits; how to find one)

3. Writing

- Project management
- Collaboration and teamwork (roles; dos and don'ts)

- Preparation
- Structure
- The needs of the reader
- Tone and style
- Redrafting: how to revise work
- Dotting the Is and crossing the Ts
- Presentation

4. Figures (diagrams and illustrations)

5. *Moving from a thesis to a book*

- The differences between thesis and book
- Practical implications for authors

6. *Keeping on the right side of the law*

7. *What next?*

- Promoting your book
- New editions
- The next book
- Building an authorial career

End matter

- Appendices (including a sample book proposal)
- Notes
- Further reading
- Index

Author

I am a Director in The Professional and Higher Partnership Ltd, which is involved in academic publishing in several ways. Please see www.professionalandhigher.com. I am currently working on projects for Sage Publications and Learning Matters. Previously I was Academic Publishing Director at the Continuum International Publishing Group Ltd. I am a Visiting Professor at Beijing Normal University and course writer for the University of Tartu. My CV and bibliography are available on request.

My first book, *Writing Successful Textbooks*, was published by A&C Black in 2001. It was reviewed very positively. The reviewer in the *TES* (22 June 2001) described the book as 'the definitive guide' and

Peter Atkins in his whole-page review in the *THES* (30 November 2001) commented that it is 'so good' that 'if aspiring authors follow his advice, the textbooks they produce should have no excuse for not being first class'.

Please note that although the proposed book covers some of the same issues as my first book, this proposal is for an entirely new work. It will incorporate some suggestions made by Peter Atkins in his *THES* review (e.g. including a section on agents).

LEVEL OF PRESENTATION AND THE MARKET FOR THE BOOK

The book will be a practical guide. Its main market consists of individual academics and the libraries that serve them. I will use examples from a range of disciplines in order to make the appeal of the book as broad as possible. There will also be some interest amongst academic managers and trainers (e.g. Staff Development Officers) and, perhaps, on Publishing Studies courses.

The issues covered in the book do not vary greatly between territories. I would therefore expect a strong market in Anglophone export markets. There is also potential in non-Anglophone markets through (a) direct sales (because many academics in these countries use English for academic purposes) and (b) translation rights. I am confident that I can obtain endorsements from abroad in order to support this potential.

The issues covered by the book will change slowly. The potential for backlist sales should therefore be strong, with the possibility of a new edition every few years.

I would expect to buy some copies for my own use.

COMPARISON WITH COMPETING BOOKS

There are numerous competing titles of which a handful are well established. These include William Germano, *From Dissertation to Book* (Chicago) and Eleanor Harman (ed.), *The Thesis and the Book* (Toronto), both of which are useful but more specialised. They are aimed purely at junior academics wanting to convert doctoral theses into monographs. In contrast, the proposed book will also help experienced academics and cover not only monographs but also trade crossover books, student guides, textbooks, and reference projects.

Amongst the established books the most direct competitors are William Germano, *Getting It Published* (Chicago, £9.50, 192 pp.) and CUP's own *Handbook for Academic Authors* by Beth Luey (£16.99, 340 pp.). My analysis of these two titles is given in the appendix to this proposal.

Overall the proposed book has several clearly distinguishing features. In particular:

1. It provides a complete treatment of what authors need to know in order to be successful. The book gives equal weight to the twin processes of writing and publication. It also includes post-publication issues.
2. The chronological structure (from deciding what to write through to producing new editions and developing an authorial career) provides a simple, coherent framework, makes for an integrated discussion, and helps the reader to read straight through from cover to cover and to retain information.
3. I include concrete, real life, examples (for example, an actual book proposal) in order to make the discussion clearer and more accessible.

CONTACT DETAILS

[Address, telephone number and e-mail address provided]
Appendix to the proposal

[I supplied the publishers with detailed analyses of the two main competing books. The analysis was organised under the following headings:

- Bibliographical details, e.g. author, title, publisher, date, extent, price
- Main strengths
- Contents
- Structure
- Treatment
- Conclusion: distinctiveness of the proposed book]

Appendix C. Guide to contracts

Framework	Date: look particularly for the commencement date.
	Parties: who is the contract between? Are the parties accurately described?
	Assignment: can the publisher assign the contract? Can you? Under what conditions?
Rights	Moral rights: look for confirmation of your moral rights and a commitment to assert them.

	Copyright	
		Ownership: who will own the copyright?
		Licence: if you are licensing rights to the publisher, how are these defined?
		Reversion: can rights revert to you? If so, under what circumstances?

Product	Extent: how long should the text be? (Seek a range, with a defined minimum and maximum.)
	Contents, including figures: what should the text contain? How many figures are required/ allowed (of what type)?
	Date: what information is there about the delivery date (for delivery of the typescript by you to the publisher) and publication date?

	Format: is there any specification about the form in which the product will be published?
	Warranties and indemnities: what do you warrant to be true? Are you certain you can provide these warranties? What are your liabilities if you break these warranties?
Process	Acceptance: how quickly will the publisher decide whether to accept your typescript and by what criteria?
	Who is going to do what and when? For example, copy-editing, proofreading, indexing.
	Control of publishing decisions: who will make decisions about, for example, the cover, the design? What entitlements do you have?
Remuneration	Who is going to pay whom?
	How much are they going to pay and on what basis?
	When will payments be made?
Meta-text (i.e. text about the contract itself).	For example, according to which country's law does it apply? How can it be terminated?

Notes

Please note that website addresses given below were correct as of 28 February 2009.

1 FOUNDATIONS

For ALCS, visit www.alcs.co.uk; for CISAC, visit www.cisac.org; for IFRRO, visit www.ifrro.org.

The *Oxford Dictionary of National Biography* is edited by H. C. G. Matthew and B. H. Harrison. The Oxford University Press website (www.oup.com/oxforddnb/info/) provides extensive information.

For soft reference series published by Blackwell, Cambridge University Press, and Oxford University Press respectively, visit www.blackwellpublishing.com (and search for 'companion'), www. cambridge.org/uk/series (and locate the series called 'Cambridge Companions ...' in the complete series listing), and www.oup.com (then search for 'Handbook').

For publications by Hackett Publishing, Channel View Publications, and the Continuum International Publishing Group respectively, visit www.hackettpublishing.com, www.multilingual-matters.com, and www.continuumbooks.com.

The best-known of the popular books written by Bertrand Russell (1872–1970) is *A History of Western Philosophy*. For a sample of the writing of Stephen Jay Gould (1941–2002), see *The Richness of Life: A Stephen Jay Gould Reader*. For Penguin Books' list, visit www.penguin. co.uk.

2 CONTEXTS

The John Donne quotation comes from 'Meditation XVII' from *Devotions upon Emergent Occasions*.

In the UK, company accounts and annual returns may be purchased online from Companies House (www.companieshouse.gov.uk). The documents referred to here are the Trustees' Report and Financial Statements for Edinburgh University Press Limited (31 July 2007) and the Abbreviated Accounts for Polity Press Limited (31 December 2006).

Susan Bassnett's article was called 'Shrinking Volumes' (*Times Higher Educational Supplement*, 10 January 2008). The address of the I. B. Tauris website is www.ibtauris.com. The announcement is taken from the 'How to publish' page. Anthony Cheetham's view of e-books is to be found in a review of Jerry Gomez's book, *Print Is Dead*, in the *Literary Review* (December 2007).

3 GETTING COMMISSIONED

The book that best explains the thinking behind commissioning decisions is Gill Davies, *Book Commissioning and Acquisition*.

For more information on grey literature, refer to the website of the Grey Literature Network Service (www.greynet.org) and to copies of the network's journal, the *Grey Journal*.

For examples of pro formas on the Internet, visit the websites of Wiley Blackwell (eu.wiley.com/WileyCDA/Section/id-302235.html) and Palgrave (www.palgrave.com/authors/publishing.asp). For Cambridge University Press's guidelines, visit authornet.cambridge.org.

An amusing, encouraging book is André Bernard, *Rotten Rejections: The Letters That Publishers Wished They'd Never Sent*.

4 CONTRACTS AND AGENTS

Carole Blake, *From Pitch to Publication*, has a very good chapter on contracts. Though it is intended for writers of fiction, much of it applies to non-fiction publishing too. Hugh Jones and Christopher Benson, *Publishing Law*, is a very well-established reference work.

A very practical book on how to negotiate in general is *Getting to Yes* by Roger Fisher and William Ury.

For The Society of Authors, visit www.societyofauthors.org. The quotation from Peter Atkins comes from 'Keep This Book to Yourself'

(*Times Higher Education Supplement*, 30 November 2001). For The
Association of Author Agents, visit www.agentsassoc.co.uk. For the
Association of Authors' Representatives, visit www.aaronline.org.

5 PROCESSES (I)

For a fuller introduction to the process view of writing, see Frank
Smith, *Writing and the Writer*.

For Tony Buzan on mind-mapping, see *Mind Mapping*. For
Edward De Bono on the positive/negative/interesting schema, see
Lateral Thinking.

6 PROCESSES (II)

Claire Kehrwald Cook's essay, 'Loose, Baggy Sentences' forms a chapter in her book, *Line by Line*. The book's sub-title, *How to Edit Your
Own Writing*, makes clear the purpose of the book. The appendix
entitled 'A Glossary of Questionable Usage' is a particularly useful
reference resource. I've come across countless authors over the years
who have benefited from this book. The quotation given here ('You
can almost detect …') comes from p. 2.

Another resource that will help you to edit your work is *Editing
and Revising Text* by Jo Billingham. Though not written specifically
for academic authors, much of the advice applies as well to academic
writing as to any other. This is an excellent resource – short, easy
to use, and entirely practical. Perhaps the chapters most relevant to
the matters discussed in Chapter 6 above are those entitled 'Editing
the Content' and 'Brevity'. If you find yourself looking at a text and
wondering, 'What do I need to do to it?', or you know what needs
to be done but don't know how to actually do it, this book may
well provide a solution. In particular, the decision trees help to guide
authors through difficulties with their texts.

I have chosen to say little in this book about specific aspects
of the English language. A number of widely available guides do
the job very well and it seems pointless to duplicate them. *The
Elements of Style* by William Strunk and E. B. White is a pocket
reference book. It features on the bibliographies of countless fresh-
man courses on composition and many people find it useful. A
more discursive book – and one that I admire – is *The Complete*

Plain Words by Ernest Gowers. This was written originally for the British civil service as an antidote to inflated, over-elaborate writing. A mid-twentieth-century text, it is inevitably (despite having been revised since) dated – yet it is not *so* dated. Any reader is likely to come away from the book with a greater awareness of language and feel for good prose. A more recent guide is *Compose Yourself* by Harry Blamires, himself an academic author. I do not understand why this lucid, concise book is little known. Its ten chapters, starting with 'Finding the Right Word' and ending with 'Reasoning and Explaining', each deal with an important aspect of composition.

On questions of grammar, I recommend without hesitation *Rediscover Grammar* by David Crystal. It is well organised, making it easy to find your way around and to dip into; the explanations are clear; and the selection of examples consistently helpful. On punctuation, *Eats, Shoots & Leaves* by Lynne Truss manages to be both informal and informative. It has proved hugely popular.

7 CRAFT

The quotations from Bertrand Russell are from the chapter entitled 'The Romantic Movement' from *History of Western Philosophy*. Those from Liz Thomas are from the chapter entitled 'The Labour Market and Participation in Post-Compulsory Education and Training' in *Widening Participation in Post-Compulsory Education*.

The quotation from I. A. Richards is from p. 182 of *Practical Criticism*. The passage from Jay Coakley is from p. 98 of *Sports in Society: Issues and Controversies*. That from Frank Dick is from p. 150 of *Sports Training Principles*.

Bjorn Gustavii, *How to Write and Illustrate a Scientific Paper*, provides detailed, practical advice on many issues, including the handling of tables and figures.

Please note that, in this chapter, I have used 'coherence' and 'cohesion' informally, without drawing a firm distinction between the two. For a discussion of the terms from the point of view of rigorous linguistics, please see Cheng Xiaotang, *Functional Approach to Discourse Coherence*.

8 DISSERTATIONS

For ProQuest's UMI Dissertation Express website, visit disexpress. umi.com/dxweb.

Of the various guides on how to progress from dissertation to book, my favourite is William Germano, *From Dissertation to Book*. It is very accessible, being both short and lucidly written. It is clearly rooted in experience and is full of sharp insights and hard-headed, practical, advice.

The Thesis and the Book, by Eleanor Harman and others, is I think less consistent and less coherent, as one might expect from an edited book. Nevertheless, it is certainly useful. Olive Holmes's chapter, 'Thesis to Book: What to Get Rid of and What to Do with What is Left', provides plenty of practical advice, and Barbara B. Reitt's chapter, 'An Academic Author's Checklist', is a useful reference tool.

Revising Your Dissertation, edited by Beth Luey, is very wide-ranging and is especially good at providing an inside view of publishing. A particular strength is that it provides detailed consideration of differences between disciplines. The chapter by Johanna E. Vondeling on publishing in professional subjects is a gem: it is wonderfully clear and concise.

For the Susan Bassnett article, please see the notes for Chapter 2 above.

9 TIME

As well as the books by Zerubavel and Bolker cited in this chapter, Robert Boice, *Professors as Writers,* is useful. It provides both short-term and long-term strategies for productive writing.

10 PEOPLE

Evelyn Ashton-Jones's essay, 'Coauthoring for Scholarly Publication: Should You Collaborate?' provides a balanced, well-organised discussion of the question raised by her sub-title. The essay appears in Moxley and Taylor, *Writing and Publishing for Academic Authors*.

The Sartre quotation comes from *Huis clos* (*No Exit*).

There is a chapter entitled 'The Publishing Process (How to Deal with Proofs)' in Robert A. Day and Barbara Gastel, *How to Write and Publish a Scientific Paper*. Though focusing on journal articles, much of the advice is applicable to books too.

In 'Responding to Reviewers' Feedback' in *Writing for Academic Journals*, Rowena Murray also focuses on journal articles, but again much of the advice applies in the case of books too.

For further information on copy-editing and proofreading, including training courses, see the Society for Editors and Proofreaders (www.sfep.org.uk). Similarly for indexing, see the Society of Indexers (www.indexers.org.uk). A standard work on book production is Marshall Lee, *Bookmaking*. Amongst the matters discussed are editing, text design, and cover design. A standard work on indexing is Nancy C. Mulvany, *Indexing Books*.

There is a wide-ranging book by Alison Baverstock entitled *Marketing Your Book: An Author's Guide*.

11 NEXT

If I could recommend one book to help authors understand the publishing industry, it would be Michael Barnard, *Transparent Imprint*. This has nothing to do with academic publishing whatsoever: it is the account of the development by Macmillan of a new fiction imprint. Its value here lies in the way that it shows how various apparently disparate aspects of publishing – commissioning, marketing, contracts, design, and so on – come together to form an integrated process. The book is in narrative form and is well written and clearly illustrated with case studies.

References

Barnard, M. *Transparent Imprint* (New York: Macmillan, 2006)

Baverstock, A. *Marketing Your Book: An Author's Guide* (London: A&C Black, 2001)

Becker, H. S. *Writing for Social Scientists: How to Start and Finish Your Thesis, Book, or Article* (University of Chicago Press, 1986)

Bernard, A. *Rotten Rejections: The Letters That Publishers Wish They'd Never Sent* (London: Robson Books, 2002)

Billingham, J. *Editing and Revising Text* (Oxford University Press, 2002)

Blake, C. *From Pitch to Publication: Everything You Need to Know to Get Your Novel Published* (Basingstoke: Macmillan, 1999)

Blamires, H. *Compose Yourself* (London: Penguin, 2003)

Boice, R. *Professors as Writers* (Stillwater, OK: New Forums Press, 1990)

Bolker, J. *Writing Your Dissertation in Fifteen Minutes a Day: A Guide to Starting* (New York: Henry and Holt, 1998)

de Bono, E. *Lateral Thinking: A Textbook of Creativity* (London: Ward Lock, 1973)

Brande, D. *Becoming a Writer* (London: Macmillan, 1996)

Buzan, T. *Mind Mapping: Kickstart Your Creativity and Transform Your Life* (Harlow: BBC, 2006)

Cheng Xiaotang, *Functional Approach to Discourse Coherence* (Beijing: Foreign Language Teaching and Research Press, 2005)

Coakley, J. *Sports in Society: Issues and Controversies*, 8th edn, International Edition (New York: McGraw-Hill, 2003)

Cook, C. K. *Line by Line: How to Edit Your Own Writing* (Boston: Houghton Mifflin, 1985)

Crystal, D. *Rediscover Grammar* (New York: Longman, 2004)

Davies, G. *Book Commissioning and Acquisition*, 2nd edn (London: Routledge, 2004)

Day, R. A., and B. Gastel, *How to Write and Publish a Scientific Paper*, 6th edn (Cambridge University Press, 2006)

Dhaliwal, S. *Making a Fortune: Learning from the Asian Phenomenon* (Chichester: Capstone, 2008)

Silent Contributors: Asian Female Entrepreneurs and Women in Business (London: Roehampton Institute, 1998)

Dick, F. W. *Sports Training Principles* (London: A&C Black, 2007)

Donne, J. *Devotions upon Emergent Occasions*, ed. A. Raspa (New York: Oxford University Press, 1987)

Fisher, J. *Ten Percent of Nothing: The Case of the Literary Agent from Hell* (Carbondale: Southern Illinois University Press, 2004)

Fisher, R., W. Ury, and B. Patton, *Getting to Yes: Negotiating Agreement without Giving In*, revised 2nd edn (London: Random House, 2003)

Germano, W. P. *From Dissertation to Book* (University of Chicago Press, 2005)

Gomez, J. *Print Is Dead: Books in Our Digital Age* (New York: Macmillan, 2007)

Gould, S. J. *The Richness of Life: A Stephen Jay Gould Reader* (New York: Vintage, 2007)

Gowers, E., S. Greenbaum, and J. Whitcut, *The Complete Plain Words*, 3rd edn (Harmondsworth: Penguin, 1987)

Gustavii, B. *How To Write and Illustrate a Scientific Paper*, 2nd edn (Cambridge University Press, 2008)

Harman, E., I. Montagnes, S. McMenemy, and C. Bucci (eds.), *The Thesis and the Book: A Guide for First-Time Academic Authors* (University of Toronto Press, 2003)

Haynes, A. *Writing Successful Textbooks* (London: A&C Black, 2001)

Jones, H., and C. Benson, *Publishing Law*, 3rd edn (Abingdon: Routledge, 2006)

Kotler, P., G. Armstrong, V. Wong, and J. Saunders, *Principles of Marketing*, 5th European edn (Harlow: Prentice Hall, 2008)

Lee, M. *Bookmaking: Editing, Design, Production*, 3rd edn (New York: W. W. Norton, 2004)

Luey, B. (ed.) *Revising Your Dissertation: Advice from Leading Editors* (Berkeley: University of California Press, 2007)

McQuail, D. *McQuail's Mass Communication Theory*, 5th edn (London: Sage, 2002)

McQuail's Reader in Mass Communication Theory (London: Sage, 2002)

Matthew, H. C. G., and B. H. Harrison, *Oxford Dictionary of National Biography Plus Index of Contributors*, 60 vols. (New York: Oxford University Press, 2004)

Moxley, J. M., and T. Taylor, *Writing and Publishing for Academic Authors*, 2nd edn (Lanham: Rowman & Littlefield, 1996)

Mulvany, N. C. *Indexing Books* (University of Chicago Press, 1994)

Murray, R. *Writing for Academic Journals* (Buckingham: Open University Press, 2004)

Samuelson, P. A., and W. D. Nordhaus, *Economics*, 18th edn (New York: McGraw-Hill, 2004)

Richards, I. A., *Practical Criticism: A Study of Literary Judgment* (London: Routledge & Kegan Paul, 1982)

Russell, B. *A History of Western Philosophy* (Woking: George Allen & Unwin, 1946)

Sartre, J.-P. *Huis clos* (New York: Routledge, 1987)

Smith, F. *Writing and the Writer* (London: Heinemann, 1982)

Strunk, W., and E. B. White, *The Elements of Style*, 4th edn (New York: Longman, 2000)

Thomas, L. *Widening Participation in Post-Compulsory Education* (London: Continuum, 2001)

Thompson, J. B. *Books in the Digital Age: The Transformation of Academic and Higher Education Publishing in Britain and the United States* (University Park, PA: Polity, 2005)

Truss, L. *Eats, Shoots & Leaves, The Zero Tolerance Approach to Punctuation!* (London: Profile Books, 2003)

Windahl, S., B. Signitzer, and J. T. Olson, *Using Communication Theory: An Introduction to Planned Communication*, 2nd edn (London: Sage, 2009)

Wood, F., and A. Sangster, *Frank Wood's Business Accounting*, 11th edn (London: Prentice Hall, 2008)

Zerubavel, E. *The Clockwork Muse: A Practical Guide to Writing Theses, Dissertations, and Books* (Cambridge, MA: Harvard University Press, 1999)

Index